FREAKY DREAMS

FREAKY DREAMS

ADELE NOZEDAR

All inquiries should be addressed to Skyhorse Publishing, 307 West 36th Street, 11th Floor, New York, NY 10018.

Skyhorse Publishing books may be purchased in bulk at special discounts for sales promotion, corporate gifts, fund-raising, or educational purposes. Special editions can also be created to specifications. For details, contact the Special Sales Department, Skyhorse Publishing, 307 West 36th Street, 11th Floor, New York, NY 10018 or info@skyhorsepublishing.com.

Skyhorse® and Skyhorse Publishing® are registered trademarks of Skyhorse Publishing, Inc.®, a Delaware corporation.

www.skyhorsepublishing.com

11 10 9 8 7 6 5 4 3 2 1

Library of Congress Cataloging-in-Publication Data available on file

Printed in China

CONTENTS

THE LAND OF NOD

I dreamed I was in the kitchen making a sandwich.
It was the weirdest dream I've ever had.

When I started researching this book, I asked people to tell me about their dreams; specifically, I was after the weirdest, the freakiest, the most disjointed examples, the ones that really do defy analysis. And the two-line quote above, was possibly one of the oddest.

It seems odd because it's so normal.

After all, it's in the nature of a dream that it's weird and freaky. If you're describing a dream to someone, is it likely that you'd ever say, "Oh my, I've got to tell you about the REALLY NORMAL dream I had last night!"? Nope!

Despite centuries of research that's still continuing, there's still so much about dreams, and indeed sleep, which remains a mystery.

Mankind has traveled into the deepest depths of the oceans. We've set foot on the moon. We've sent probes to pick up pebbles from Mars, and we've taken photographs in the unfathomable vastness of space. And yet we still don't know quite what happens, or where we go to, every night when we toddle off to bed, close our eyes, and sleep.

For example, here's something that's very puzzling.

If you've ever watched someone sleeping, you might have noticed their eyeballs moving swiftly back and forth under the lids. This is called Rapid Eye Movement (REM), and it happens when the sleeper is dreaming. Dreams are our way of processing the events of the day, incidents in our lives, and all sorts of physical and philosophical phenomena.

The duck-billed platypus, of all animals on earth, shows the most extreme incidence of REM.

What is the platypus processing? What sort of anxieties could exist in that little platypus mind? We'll never know. Another mystery. In fact, to be fair, scientists aren't even certain that the platypus is even dreaming.

BUT WHAT IF IT IS?

The great thing about dreams is that anything can happen, any kind of surreal scenario is allowed to play out, no holds barred. In your dream world, you can be a superhero or a god, an animal, a tramp, a teapot. Dreams allow us to tap into an internal imaginary world that is as vast as that external universe that the space probes poke around in. The possibility of a fabulous dream is enough to make bedtime seem like a really fun proposition.

HOW TO REMEMBER YOUR DREAMS

The dream is the small hidden door in the deepest and most intimate sanctum of the soul, which opens into that primeval cosmic night that was soul long before there was a conscious ego and will be soul far beyond what a conscious ego could ever reach.
-Carl Jung, *The Meaning of Psychology for Modern Man*, 1934

We're presupposing that you already know how to sleep, so let's get straight to the juicy stuff. Some of us really do believe that we never dream, or maybe that we dream only very rarely.

That's not true. Everyone dreams.
What's more, we each have several episodes of dreaming throughout the night. They occur primarily during the period of REM described above, during which our most intense dreams take place, but there's also a phase called Non-Rapid Eye Movement (NREM) during which dreams might happen—or they might not..

So, if we all dream, then why don't we all remember them?

Some scientists have speculated that we don't remember them simply because it wouldn't be healthy to do so. After all, if we had to think not only of all the stuff that happens every day in our waking lives AND then think about our dreams, we'd probably go mad. There also needs to be a clear distinction between dreams and waking reality. For example, to dream of flinging yourself from the top of a moving train and then finding that you can fly to safety is fine, but to try the same thing in real life wouldn't be very clever. Dreams are by their very nature full of absurd scenarios and impossible situations which would simply never happen in our waking lives.

Always with the adjunct "Safety First," then, here are some tips on how to remember your dreams.

DECIDE TO REMEMBER YOUR DREAMS

Start out by making the decision that you do actually want to be able to recall your dreams. Tell yourself that this is what you want. Repeat this mantra several times a day:

I will remember my dreams.
I will remember my dreams.
I will remember my dreams.

BREAK UP YOUR SLEEP PATTERN

If you can, aim to break up your sleep pattern. We remember our dreams usually when we've been woken up in the middle of, or immediately after, a dream episode.

You might have a dedicated friend who will time how long it take between you falling asleep until the REM pattern starts. You could try setting an alarm to wake yourself when this happens. Otherwise, try setting the alarm at random times. We sleep in 90-minute cycles, so if you don't have to get up at the crack of dawn the next day, you could set an alarm clock to go off at 90-minute intervals throughout the night.

Other ways of breaking up your sleep pattern include eating indigestible food (see "Cheese Dreams" on page 50), taking a long-haul flight into another time zone, or having a baby.

RECORD THE DREAM

The tried and tested method is to have a notebook and (working) pen or pencil beside the bed, but you might prefer to have a recording device. Remember, after all, that Keith Richards recorded "Satisfaction" in his sleep. Whatever means you decide to use, make sure they're easily accessible and that you're familiar with any technology. Dreams can be extraordinarily elusive and could easily escape by the time you've jabbed away at the paper with a succession of useless pens, or worked out which button to push.

REMIND YOURSELF OF WHAT YOU'RE DOING

It's easy, befuddled with sleep, to forget what your aim is, especially if you're trying the 90-minute alarm clock method. It's all too simple to simply throw the clock across the room and continue snoozing. You might try placing a piece of card with the words "REMEMBER DREAM!" somewhere that you'll see as soon as you wake up.

DON'T TRY TO ANALYZE ANYTHING

It's more important that you get the details down without immediately worrying about the meaning of them. Let the dreams "be." Let them breathe, live with them a little while before deconstructing them.

While you're at it, you might want to consider using your dreams to solve problems.

You'll see several examples dotted through this book about ingenious solutions that have been found in a dream, delivered to the dreamer as though on a silver platter. If you have any sort of conundrum, think of it several times during the day and then concentrate on it before you go beddybyes. See what happens. By the way, you're more likely to have pleasant dreams if you're close to a pleasant scent, and vice versa.

A DISCLAIMER

Although the bulk of this book is an analysis of some of the features that might appear in your dreams, some of the freakiest dreams are simply beyond explanation, pure and simple. Don't worry if this is the case with one of your dreams. Enjoy it, revel in it, have a laugh about it.

IN CONCLUSION

If you take all this into consideration and start to apply it, you'll find that the more you remember your dreams, the easier it will get. It's almost as though your subconscious mind, knowing that you're extending the hand of friendship, starts to come out to play and communicate with you.

YOU MIGHT SEE PATTERNS EMERGING.

YOU MIGHT DREAM OF AN INVENTION THAT MAKES YOU A MILLIONAIRE.

YOU MIGHT INVENT A PLOT THAT TURNS INTO A BEST-SELLING BOOK.

WHATEVER YOU DO, YOU'LL DEFINITELY HAVE FUN.

ENJOY YOUR FREAKY DREAMS!

"READ THE DIRECTIONS AND DIRECTLY YOU WILL BE DIRECTED IN THE RIGHT DIRECTION."

The Doorknob, *Alice's Adventures in Wonderland*

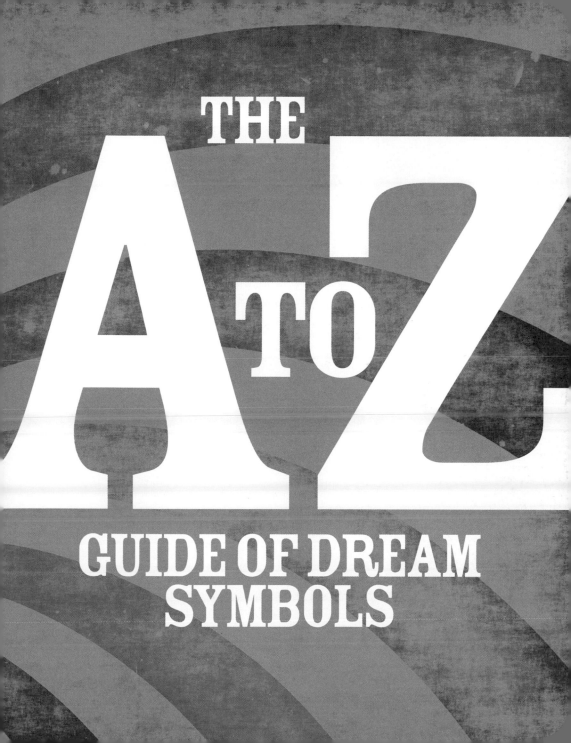

THE A TO Z

GUIDE OF DREAM
SYMBOLS

There are many wonderful books full of dream symbols. Then there are also some real doozies. In general, a symbol represents itself. For example, let's say that you dream about a lion. Then you have to ask yourself—what is a lion? A big shaggy animal with golden hair, pointy teeth, and sharp claws that comes from Africa? Is it the symbol for one of the astrological signs? Or is it an animal that represents courage, strength, fortitude, and ferocity? Then again, you might immediately think of the cowardly lion in the *Wizard of Oz*. The lion is, of course, all of these things and more. If you dream of a lion, then the meaning of the dream is dictated by what the lion means to you, personally, as well as the archetypal meaning of the symbol and the context in which it actually appears in the dream. It's not always easy, but here at Freaky Dreams Central we like to apply the principle of Ockham's Razor to just about everything. What is Ockham's Razor? Aside from being a fabulous phrase to throw in at fancy dinner parties, Ockham's Razor means that of all the possible explanations for everything under the sun, the simplest and most obvious one is generally the best.

ABBREVIATIONS

Inspect your dreams carefully. They are full of hidden messages. When you spot an abbreviation, see if there's a possibility that it might stand for something. For example, the abbreviation could be the initials of a person. Roman numerals might constitute a date. XL could translate as the word "excel." You get the idea.

ABYSS

This can indicate the depths of your subconscious mind—maybe you're afraid of facing up to something that you know you have to deal with sooner rather than later. It could also mean that there's a "plunge" to be taken, like some kind of a cosmic bungee jump. Bear in mind that scary stuff can also be incredibly exciting, so an abyss in a dream isn't necessarily a bad omen.

ACCIDENT

If you dream that you're involved in an accident, it's likely that there is a situation in your life that you're not happy with; perhaps a metaphorical "accident waiting to happen." To dream that you're the cause of an accident is a good example of the common anxiety dream. Look to see what you're worried about in your waking life and make moves to change things. If you dream that someone in your life has been in an accident, it could mean that you are genuinely worried for that person or it could mean that it's time for your relationship with them to come to an end. Only you can know which answer is likely to be correct.

ACORN

A new beginning, the germ of an idea, something that's going to be BIG. Stick with it. You're inspired!

ADULATION

It's likely that you've done something that you're very pleased with—a project at work, perhaps or a new idea or invention you've devised. Your dream of adulation confirms this. However, it's also possible that the world is not giving you the encouragement you need and that your subconscious mind needs to make up for it while you're asleep.

ADULTERY

If you dream about adultery, it's all down to the context. If you're committing adultery in your dream, it's possible that your marriage is in need of some close scrutiny. Perhaps you're bored and need to spice things up. If your partner is committing adultery in your dream, again your marriage could be in need of some close scrutiny because of boredom factors. Or perhaps you're afraid that they might be hiding something—a lover, perhaps, but not necessarily.

ALARM CLOCK

Most of our dreams are, unfortunately, related to anxiety, and a dream about an alarm clock falls into this category. We set alarms when we want to be woken up; this could be physically or metaphorically. Clocks also indicate an obsession with time; maybe you feel you're running out of the stuff or you're trying to meet a deadline.

ALBATROSS

The definitive interpretation of the albatross's symbolism is best summed up in "The Rime of the Ancient Mariner" by Samuel Taylor Coleridge. In this epic poem, he writes:
"Instead of the cross, the albatross About my neck was hung."
Because of the mythology of the albatross as something that hinders you, this dream symbol is more than the sum of its realistic parts. Not just any old sea bird, the albatross represents the idea of something holding you back. And if it appears in your dreams, then this might correlate with a similar situation in your real life.

ALBINO

Anything albino is something that has no color pigmentation, something that's purely white. White is symbolic of purity, so it could be reflective of something in your life that is pure or innocent. But there is also something very different about an albino since it's not something we are accustomed to seeing in our everyday lives. To see anything albino in your dream could also suggest that there is an aspect of your waking life in which you feel different or alienated.

ALCOHOL

Alcohol changes our state of mind; we drink it, we sometimes get drunk, we become happy or sad or maybe angry, sometimes we dance on tables, and sometimes we fall over. Alcohol enables us to lose our inhibitions and perhaps your booze-laden dream is telling you to let your hair down a little in your everyday life?

ALIEN

What constitutes an alien? Is it a small green creature with slanted, expressionless black eyes? Is it a foreigner? Is it the feeling of being a stranger in a strange land? Of course, it's all of these, and more. An alien in your freaky dream could suggest you're feeling disconnected, divorced from reality and the people around you. New experiences are exciting but also scary, and you might be dreaming of aliens if this is your current situation in life. To be abducted by aliens means that circumstances are out of your control.

ALMOND

The defining quality of the almond is the incredibly tough exterior that hides its sweet and tender meat. The dream almond might represent you, or another person with these qualities. It could also be something in your life that requires a lot of effort to attain the result you need. Incidentally, almonds are also a symbol of fertility as well as of marriage. This symbolism goes for nuts in general.

ANCESTOR

Your ancestry is effectively a bank of genetic factors, character traits, diseases, talents, ingenuity, and potential. You are at the end of a long line of such a train, which represents the infinite capacity of your own potential. This is exciting, but when there are endless possibilities, it can also be difficult to make a decision about which choice to make. Is indecision a dilemma that you're facing? If you see one of your ancestors in a dream, then he or she appears as a reminder of your own skills and genetic disposition. Thinking about the talents you've inherited from that ancestor might help you make a decision.

ANCHOR

The symbolism of the anchor is obvious; stability and security. However anchors can also hold you down. So what is the anchor like in your dream? Again, it's all about context and the feeling of the dream.

ANCIENT CIVILIZATION

If you ever dreamed that you were in the midst of a glamorous ancient civilization, this rarefied and exotic environment probably means that your everyday, waking life has become somewhat humdrum, and you're in dire need of an injection of mystery, color, excitement—and a touch of the unknown.

ANGEL

This angel is a powerful archetypal symbol, known and recognized all over the planet. You don't have to be religious to know what an angel is all about. And the more powerful a place that a particular symbol enjoys in our psyche, the more powerful its meaning within your dream.

Angels, though, are full of contradictions. They can be sweet, loving, and gentle. Or they can be stern masters of discipline. They can help us, or they can teach us the hardest lessons. They can create and destroy in equal measure.

Above all, the angel is a messenger. Now, if you do believe in God, then it's likely that you'll see the angel in your dream as carrying information directly from the Head Office, so to speak. However, others believe that we carry our "God" inside of ourselves, but we don't always listen to the messages conveyed by this internal authority, who knows instinctively and intuitively what's right and wrong in the context of the bigger picture.

Therefore, you should pay close attention to any angel that appears in your dream, since it's likely to be giving you information; it doesn't matter where you think the source of this information lies. This information may be direct—the angel may speak to you—or it could be indirect, for example, if the angel is holding a scroll, indicating hidden information that you'll need to decipher.

It's possible that you might even dream that you, yourself, are an angel. This could be a reminder that you have a great capacity to help others, or that you are more powerful than you think.

ANIMALS

Individual species of animals—such as dogs, cats, or horses—appear under their own names in this book. However, it's also worth examining the meaning of animal dreams in general. The animal side of human beings speaks to intuition and instinct, the primitive, the sexual. Sometimes if we're feeling repressed, an animal dream might allow us to feel that we have more freedom than we're able to express in our everyday lives. Don't forget, too, that animals show us more than just our primitive desires. Many cultures believe that we each have "totem" animals—that is, that we share

aspects and characteristics of certain creatures. The best way that this is expressed is in the zodiacs of both Western and Eastern astrology, whose animal shapes parade around the skies. So, to dream of an animal is to be shown that you share the qualities of that creature, whether they seem to be scary, freaky, or perfectly normal.

ANKH

Although this symbol originally belonged to the ancient Egyptians, its meaning is universally accepted; it stands for eternal life. To see it in a dream is a reminder of the connectedness of all things.

APE

Dreams often contain visual or literal puns; bear in mind that to "ape" someone means to copy them. Perhaps you're worried about this in some context? If not, the ape is also powerful and sexually driven but also known to be undignified and somewhat stupid. Ring any bells for you?

APOCALYPSE

Many dreams—or nightmares—have an apocalyptic theme or feel to them. It's likely that such a dream reflects similar changes in your life (where one part of your life is coming to an end), although hopefully these changes are not quite so dramatically intense as an actual apocalypse! Such changes might include moving house, marriage or divorce, or a change of job. The apocalypse dream is a prime example of how dreams tend to exaggerate events in our lives and amplify our anxieties.

APPLAUSE

Dreaming of a large auditorium of people applauding you is a relatively common dream and usually a pleasant one. Dreams sometimes give us an experience we're lacking in real life, though, so it's probable that you're not receiving the recognition you really deserve.

APPLE

Ever since Eve offered Adam the Fruit of Knowledge—commonly supposed to be the apple—this fruit has occupied an important place as a premium symbol. Accordingly, to dream about the apple is to dream about wisdom, information, knowledge, healthiness, and prosperity. The apple, because of its seeds, is also a fertility symbol. Do you have fertility issues, either positive or negative?

Conversely, to see an apple rotting on a bough is a powerful symbol of autumn and mortality. It could be a reminder that life is short and to "use it or lose it."

APRON

Aprons protect, but there's more to this than you might suppose. Yes, they protect a person's clothes from splashes and stains while working, but aprons also protect and preserve secrets. Freemasons, for example, use the apron as part of their uniform. If you're dreaming of aprons, it could be there is a secret you're keeping or one that is being kept from you.

ARCH

To dream that you are traveling underneath an arched structure signifies a portentous moment in your life, a new beginning, and something good to come.

ARROW

The basic arrow speaks of direction, focus, and enthusiasm in your life. A broken arrow signifies the opposite; the end of a dream or a fear of failure.

ASTEROID

This signifies an illuminating episode, such as a sudden flash of clarity or creativity—a "eureka" moment!

ASTRONAUT

What do astronauts do? They travel into outer space. In a spirit of exploration. In a spaceship...OK, but what do they REALLY do? Of course; they reach for the stars. This is what you're doing. Good luck!

ATTACK

Assuming that you're not a prize fighter or similar in your waking life, if you dream that you're attacking someone, then you could be suffering from unreleased anger or pent-up frustration. If, however, you are being attacked, then it's likely that you're suffering from a lack of self-confidence or certainty, or that you're being bullied in your waking life. This dream is telling you to face up to these attackers.

ATTIC

As a part of a house (in which the different rooms represent different aspects of ourselves), the attic represents the head, the mind, the intellect—and the higher, spiritual self. Therefore, finding yourself in an attic is a great opportunity to discover the condition of your thought processes. If, for example, you feel nervous or troubled in this dream attic, then you might decide to look into the way you think about things in your life.

AUTOPSY

If there is a dead body being dissected in your dream, then you've managed to find yourself at an autopsy. This dream indicates that you are similarly dissecting a situation in your waking life which is irretrievable, but which can still be taken as an opportunity for learning. Take the information you need and then walk away from the corpse.

AVALANCHE

A series of emotions, held back, are now coming to the forefront and need to be expressed, by any means necessary. Alternatively, you might feel overwhelmed by a series of events in your life. Either way, you should regard the avalanche as a positive signal.

BABY

There are, of course, many different ways in which a baby might appear in your dream. In essence, a baby represents new potential as well as fragility, something which needs to be protected and allowed to grow. In this case, the baby could even represent something as simple as a new idea or recently discovered talent. However, if you are actually pregnant, such a dream might be your own way of expressing anxiety about the new life that's inside you and the changes that it will bring to your life. If you dreamed that you had a baby that you'd forgotten about, then the baby represents a part of you, yourself, that you have neglected and that now wants attention. If the baby in your dream is dead, it signifies the failure of an idea.

BADGER

Remember that dreams offer us information in all sorts of ways, sometimes in puns. To "badger" someone is to doggedly try to persuade them of something. Maybe this is happening to you or you're doing it to someone else? The badger itself is also a symbol of hard work, determination, and stubbornness. If there is someone in your life who is set in their ways, then the badger in your dream could represent that person.

BAG

Think about the bag in your dream. Is it intriguing and full of different pockets, some of them ingeniously hidden? Then this indicates the many different "compartments" of your psyche and includes your hidden desires and ambitions yet to be fulfilled. If the bag is too heavy, then perhaps the metaphorical burden that you're carrying in real life is similarly overloaded. If the bag is empty, it's likely that you have a very "zen" attitude toward life and eschew material possessions.

BAKERY (BAKING)

Baking or a bakery signifies riches, success, satisfaction, and gain in all areas. Bread means money, and so does dough, right? Enjoy.

BALD

With a baldness dream, context is all. If you're a man with a full head of hair dreaming that you're bald, this could constitute an anxiety dream. This could be anxiety about actually going bald or anxiety about a different situation in your life. If you're a woman in a similar position, multiply that anxiety times ten. If you're already bald, however, dreaming of this condition is a reminder of your own wisdom.

BALL

You might be seeing a basic soccer ball in your dream, but it's likely to have a more profound meaning than a simple piece of sports equipment. Dreams often play with imagery, and the shape of the globe suggests completion and wholeness; the Universe, no less. If you are watching a ball game and not participating, it could mean that you need to overcome insecurity or anxiety in your waking life. If you are at a costume ball, then be wary of someone close to you who doesn't have your best interests at heart.

BANANA

The saucy banana, appearing in a dream, is a not-very-well-disguised phallic symbol. You could either be unhealthily obsessed with them or repressing certain sexual urges. You can also slip on banana skins, so do be careful.

BANK

Generally speaking, the bank dream is about security—and not just the financial kind. A bank is somewhere that we put things to keep them safe, so you need to determine what you feel is being threatened that needs security. A relationship? Your job? Context is all when you have this dream. If you dream that you're robbing a bank, maybe you feel that you're not receiving the credit you deserve in your waking life and need to grasp it for yourself.

BANQUET

Generally speaking, food and eating represent spiritual nourishment rather than the bodily kind. If you dream that you're taking part in a banquet or a feast, it's possible that you're not getting the sort of spiritual satisfaction that you crave in your "normal" life. Then again, if you're following a strict diet or regime in your waking life, then it's possible that the dream is compensating for all the treats you're missing; your subconscious is "cheating" on your diet.

BARE FEET

If you don't usually go barefoot in your everyday life, how does it feel to go barefoot in your dream? If you feel nervous or uncomfortable, the bare feet could indicate that you feel exposed about someone or something. After all, footwear protects an important part of our body. If, on the other hand, going barefoot feels liberating and lovely, then the dream is indicating that you need to let your hair down once in a while and try something new. You might even like it!

FAMOUS FREAKY DREAMERS
THE SWINGING SPORTSMAN

Jack Nicklaus is one of the worlds' most famous and successful golfers, but in the mid 1960s his play wasn't on form and he had run into a bad patch of scores. It was after a dream that his luck finally turned around. Here's what happened, as reported in the San Francisco Chronicle on June 27,1964:

On Wednesday night I had a dream and it was about my golf swing. I was hitting them pretty good in the dream and all at once I realized I wasn't holding the club the way I've actually been holding it lately. I've been having trouble collapsing my right arm taking the club head away from the ball, but I was doing it perfectly in my sleep. So when I came to the course yesterday morning I tried it the way I did in my dream and it worked. I shot a sixty-eight yesterday and a sixty-five today.

BAT

It's not really surprising that the bat has a reputation for evil and devilishness. It looks pretty sinister, after all, swooping around in the dark with pointy wings and beady eyes. Of course, the bat is also associated with all things demonic—including, of course, vampires. If bats appear in your dream, it can signify irritations and hindrances as well as the other "horror movie" symbolism suggested above.

BATHING

Immersion in water has a deep spiritual meaning and is an important ritual in many faiths all over the world. To dream of bathing isn't just about cleansing the body, but also the soul— letting go of the past, washing away any stagnant areas in your life, and letting new ideas flow.

BEACH

Funny places, beaches. They're not quite land, and yet not quite water. The beach goes into the water, and the water laps up onto the beach, the sand a no-man's land between the two elements. Therefore, the beach is considered a liminal place, a threshold between two worlds. This probably reflects your current situation. You could be between jobs, relationships, or homes. Beaches of course also signify vacations and holidays, a time away from the normal routines of life, so the dream could be your way of taking a mental vacation.

BEADS

Beads (and buttons) indicate that you need to be patient. Is there an aspect of your life that seems slow at the moment? Remember that you can achieve a great deal in tiny steps—like the effort taken to string beads into a necklace. To dream of a broken string of beads is a common anxiety dream, particularly so if the beads don't belong to you.

BEAR

If you're being chased by a bear, it could be that you're afraid to address the bearlike side of yourself; after all, with power comes responsibility. If you're wrestling with a bear, then two sides of your nature are at odds with one another. It's also possible that you're being forced to do something that is against your moral principles. A bear is a powerful totem animal, if you're interested in that aspect of your dreams. Dreaming of one could mean you have access to all the power and might of the bear and you share its qualities.

BED

This is where we do most of our freaky dreaming, right? Therefore, to find yourself dreaming about a bed might seem to be a curious waste of good sleep time. However, a bed is where the majority of acts of love take place, so maybe your dream hints toward more carnal matters. If the bed is well made in your dream, then this indicates that your life is in order. If it's disheveled and scruffy, though, the opposite is true. If you can't find your bed at all, then your dream is one of anxiety. Is there anyone else in the bed? If it's a sexy stranger, then maybe your waking life needs to be perked up a little.

BEDBUGS

These microscopically tiny little critters are just something we have to live with since we can't seem to get rid of them. Dreaming of bedbugs could be a reminder about a pesky and relentless situation in your own life, perhaps a problem that just won't get resolved. If your dream bedbugs have attained an alarming size, then this dream is giving you one clear message: don't sweat the small stuff. See your troubles for what they are, as inconsequential and as inevitable as bedbugs.

BED-WETTING

Is it you that's reverted back to this infantile behavior? This sort of dream leaves the dreamer feeling humiliated and wretched. You could be feeling that you have a lack of control in your real life, that situations are being thrust upon you that you're not ready for. It could be that you're taking on too much. Also, a bed-wetting dream is a typical anxiety dream, so you need to alleviate whatever those anxieties might be in your waking life.

BEES

Archetypal symbols of industry and harmonious cooperation, dreaming about bees could be a congratulatory reminder that you are applying the same principles in your waking life—or conversely, they could be sending you a signal that certain attitudes of your could be improved upon.

BESOM (*See* Broom)

BESTIALITY

Whoa! If you're dreaming about having sex with an animal, then this qualifies as truly freaky. What sort of an animal is it? What part are you playing? Is it fun, or are you on the receiving end of something way too big and scary? Before you make an appointment with your therapist, it's important to remember that animals in dreams represent a hidden side of ourselves and the symbolism is fairly obvious; a tiger for ferocity, a deer for gentleness and fragility, a rabbit for sexuality, for example. Embrace whatever the creature is, as a part of you that needs attention.

BIRD

Like the industrious bee, the bird is an important archetypal symbol, and having one appear in your dream can

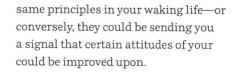

have profound meaning. Anything with wings can move in a different dimension and so were considered, like angels, to be messengers from the gods themselves. But how to translate that message? First, try to identify the bird. A water bird, for example, speaks of hidden depths; literally, there's more beneath the surface than you might imagine. A large air bird such as a condor can see great distances and can assess situations almost before they happen. A flock of dark birds might seem threatening, as though you're being beset with problems that deny you a clear vision of what's ahead. If you're flying with birds, then you are liberated and joyful, happy in your life.

BLOG

If you dream that you're writing a blog, this could be a sign that you need to take more control of events in your life. It's also possible that in your waking life you're spending more time in front of a screen than is considered healthy. Live your life actively instead of playing it out on your laptop!

BLOOD

An essential component of our health, the bright red color of our blood is symbolic of life itself. If you dream that blood is splattered all over the place, then your dream is straying into nightmare territory. It could be an accurate reflection of violence in your own life, but it's more commonly a signal of anxiety. If you find yourself drinking blood in your dream, it might be that there's a similar situation in your life; something that you're trying to hide, a guilty secret. If you see blood pouring away down a river or into a drain, then you are feeling that your life forces are being washed away. Look to the state of your physical health.

BOSS

The meaning of a "boss" dream depends on your relationship with your own boss. It could indicate that you have problems with authority figures or that you're spending too much time obsessing about work. Alternatively, an authority figure in a dream is sometimes there to offer guidance that's needed by our subconscious mind, so listen to whatever your boss is telling you in the dream. It's also worth considering that your "boss" might even be your husband, wife, or partner—or perhaps your child.

BOTTLE

Any dream about a container is about the container that is you. Is the bottle transparent or opaque? Is it full or is it empty? If it is full, then you're feeling fortunate and all is fine. If it's empty, you're feeling drained and tired, with nothing left to give. If it's a champagne bottle that you're dealing with, then there's something to celebrate or there will be soon; celebrate yourself!

BOUGH (See Branch)

BOUND

If you're tied up or bound in any way, this could be a Freudian dream of sexual repression. It's equally likely that you're feeling restricted in other areas of your life, too.

BOX

Like the bottle, this is a "container" dream. The box represents you. So, whether the box is open or shut, and whether it's full or empty, will speak to you about where you are in your life at this particular moment. If the box is full of flowers, that's a positive sign. If, on the other hand, it's full of wriggly creepy-crawlies, then maybe you need to think some things through. You could be keeping a secret or repressing something. Above all, remember what happened to Pandora.

BRA

If you're a woman dreaming of a shabby old bra, you're feeling neglected and unappreciated. After all, a woman's breasts are an important symbol of sexuality, motherhood, and femininity. If you dream of a sexy, lacy bra, you're feeling confident about your feminine side in particular, and about life in general. If you're a man dreaming of skimpy lingerie, you might be lacking physical love in your waking life.

BRANCH

Branches and boughs can refer to your family. If they're broken, perhaps there's a similar breakdown in communications or even a death. Healthy, leafy branches can suggest encouraging news, new growth, or fresh ideas—they could even act as a prophesy dream indicating a new "branch" to the family in the form of a marriage or a baby.

BREAD

The staff of life, the loaf represents the basic needs in life. Not simply material —although bread is a euphemism for money—it can stand for spiritual sustenance, too. The sliced white bread that you dream of could be a reminder that you need to address your soul as well as your body.

BREASTS

Breasts speak of maternal nourishment but are equally valid as symbols of sexual desire and arousal. If you're a straight female and get turned on by a dream of glamour-model-perfect breasts, don't be alarmed by such a reminder of your own sexuality. Dreams know no boundaries.

BRIDGE

Like the beach, the bridge symbolizes a state between two places, a suspension in the air between two landmasses. It could be that there's a similar "bridge situation" playing out in your own life at the moment: a wedding (two families about to join), or a transitional time between homes, relationships, or jobs. Should your dream bridge be broken or otherwise precarious, the dream is simply helping you to express your own anxiety about the situation.

BROOM

(Or brush or besom) signifies the need for a clean sweep; not necessarily the domestic kind, but a clearing out of your life. Sweep away the dead wood! A hairbrush carries a similar meaning.

BRUSH (See Broom)

BUTTERFLY

In many cultures, the butterfly symbolizes the soul. Has someone died, or is someone about to be born? This soul could be bringing you a message. The Red Admiral butterfly that you dream about could be a reminder of this. But the butterfly is also a lighthearted creature, flitting from flower to flower, seemingly not taking anything too seriously. Its appearance could be a reminder that you might apply that same carefree attitude in your own life.

BUTTONS (See Beads)

CAGE

Some dream symbols are disguised, but sometimes they're ridiculously obvious. A cage, of course, signifies a feeling of entrapment, restriction, and confinement. The frustrations and inhibitions imposed upon you by the cage could be to do with your work situation, your home situation, and your relationships.

CALENDAR

If you see a calendar in a dream, try to remember if you were shown a particular date. Bear in mind that the numbers and months might be scrambled. If no dates were shown, the calendar is indicating the passing of time. It could be that you're working toward a deadline or that you're worried that time is running out in a particular area of your life.

CAMERA

If you're using the camera in your dream, then it could be indicating you need to look at things in a different way or that you need to look at something in more detail. If, however, someone is taking a picture of you, then it's likely that you're worried about the way you appear to others.

CANDLE

To dream about any kind of light source is a good, happy symbol. It means you are enjoying a time of illumination, and the dream is reminding you of that. If the candle is snuffed, however, then you might be having problems trying to get people to understand your point of view.

CANNIBALS

If there are cannibals in your dream, it's probable that you will be trying to escape from them. The larger percentage of dreams stem from anxiety, and that would include the prospect of being boiled alive and served up as a stew! If you are invited to the cannibals' feast, however, you'll be asked to swallow something unacceptable. Does this reflect a situation in your waking life? If so, make moves to change that situation.

CAPE

If you're wearing a cape, cloak, or any other similar covering, then you have something to hide.

CAR

An interesting dream to have, and there are lots of things you need to ask yourself. If you're driving the car, then it means you're in charge of your destiny. If someone else is driving the car, then someone else is the boss in your life. If you're happy to be the passenger, then that is fine; if not, then the dream suggests that there is an imbalance in a close relationship.

If the car is rolling smoothly along the road, then you're literally on an easy ride. If it's bumpy, the opposite is true and you can expect to have to overcome some obstacles. If a car is broken down in real life, we expect delays and frustrations; in the dream, the same is true. Keep in mind that when something doesn't go according to plan and we find ourselves unable to do anything but wait, we can be forced to think about things and perhaps find solutions to certain situations. If your dream car is broken down, then this could be your dream telling you to take time out, see things differently, and reflect on your life.

CASTLE

Goody! If you dream of a castle, then well-deserved praise and adulation is due to you. Real life and dreams don't always match up, though; if your bank balance isn't boosted within a few days, the dream still indicates you accomplished something noteworthy.

CASTRATION

If you're a man and you dream of this, then chances are you feel that your creative forces are at an all-time low. If you're a woman dreaming that you're castrating a man, then the most obvious interpretation is that there's a man in your life that needs to be taken down a peg or two!

CAT

Generally speaking, the cat is the symbol of feminine wisdom, mystery, hidden knowledge, and information. Bear in mind that animals in dreams often remind us about forgotten aspects of ourselves, and the feminine aspect of the pussycat can apply to male as well as female dreamers— guys, perhaps you need to get in touch with your female feline side? As well as belonging to witches, a black cat crossing your path is a symbol of bad luck in some places like the U.S., so it could be mirroring some difficult times in your life. In other places like the U.K., black cats are symbols of good luck, so it's considered a good omen to dream of one there. If the cat in your dream is friendly, then your own catlike qualities are nicely integrated in your personality. If the cat is unfriendly or hostile, on the other hand, then it could indicate that you are neglecting your pussycat side.

CATERPILLAR

The caterpillar in your dream is telling you there is a long way to go before you get what you need to fulfill your true potential. But since this journey is all part of a natural process, the caterpillar dream is not a negative one.

CAVE

A cave, a fissure, an underground chamber or anything along those lines signifies the womb, and to find yourself inside a cave indicates a metaphorical return to the womb. You will go through a process of meditation or self-reflection followed by a glorious rebirth.

CELEBRITIES

Like it or not, our celebrities are not simply "normal" human beings. Their perceived traits, accurate or not, become amplified both by the media and our own personal perceptions. Therefore, if a celebrity or other public figure appears in your dream, then he or she represents whatever you believe those people to be. These are all qualities that are available to you

whether you see them as good or bad; charm, irritability, beauty, sexiness, unattractiveness; it's impossible to name every single celebrity and their characteristics that might appear to you while you're asleep, but you get the general idea. If you dream of a celebrity that you admire, then those admirable qualities can be a part of yourself. If, on the other hand, your dream celebrity is a nightmare of vainglorious egomania and insufferably annoying behavior, you might want to check your own behavior for similar traits.

CELLAR

If the house represents yourself, then the cellar represents that part of you which is underground, buried, or beneath the surface; that is, your subconscious mind. If the cellar in your dream is dank, untidy, and slightly scary, then you need to pay attention to what's going on in your subconscious mind and bear in mind that dreams are its way of communicating with you! If, on the other hand, the cellar is pleasant and a place that you're happy to spend time in, then rest assured that all is well with your subconscious mind. It's not unlikely that you're involved in a spiritual practice such as meditation or yoga. The cellar can also represent the past; you might have issues from a previous life that you need to reconcile with your current one.

CHALK

Where is chalk used the most? In a school environment. So if someone is writing something on a chalkboard in your dream, you're being taught something by this person. If you're using chalk, then you are learning something. If you can discern that you're reading or what you're writing, then you're fortunate indeed. Don't forget, though, that dream information is often cleverly encrypted. And that chalk is impermanent...

CHAMBER (See Cave)

CHECKERBOARD (CHESSBOARD)

The black and white squares of a checkerboard represent a balance of opposites. The contrasting colors, shared equally on the board, represent good and bad, light and dark, and the essential contrast between them. It's for this reason that, for example, Masonic lodges often have black and white checkered floors. It's likely that you have a clear, black and white decision to make in your own life.

CHEETAH

Animals and dreams signify power that's available to us. The cheetah is fast and strong. Go for it.

CHERRY

Any kind of fruit tends to be a good omen in a dream, but only if the fruit is fresh and perky. In addition, a cherry has the inevitable sexual connotations. What's the context of the cherry in your dream? If you're eating the cherry, then your sex life is healthy and interesting. If you're seeing someone else eating the cherry, this could indicate you're frustrated in your sex life. If you see a bowl of cherries, then it is a reminder that life is sweet. However, if you see a bowl of cherry stones, it means that you're expending too much energy and need to ease up a little.

CHICKEN

Traditionally, we associate chickens with cowardice. Are you being less than courageous in a certain aspect of your life? If so, take heart and know that you can change things for the better.

CHIMPANZEE (See Monkey)

CLOTHING

Any kind of clothing that features in a dream tells us about the way we'd like to appear to the world—and also about the way we'd like the world to see us. What kind of a jacket is it? Is it a formal, tailored jacket? Or is it more casual, even bordering on scruffy? Does it feel comfortable? Or does the cut of the cloth make you feel uneasy? The type of clothes in your dream will illustrate how you want yourself to appear to the people around you.

CLOWN

For all their jolly jests, clowns can have a quite sinister appearance. The most alienating aspect is the strange face paint that is as effective as a mask; the clown is unidentifiable, which in itself sets a tone of danger. The clown in your dream might well represent someone that pretends to be something that they're not, or that you can't quite get a grip on. If the clown in your dream is unhappy or sad, then you need to think about if this perhaps applies to you or someone in your life?

COCKEREL

The cockerel is a powerful symbol of masculine aggression and virility. It's also a symbol of the power of the sun. These are all qualities that, according to your dream, are available to you.

CHEESE DREAMS: DOES FOOD MAKE FREAKY DREAMS...FREAKIER?

Does eating cheese actually make us dream more, or is this just an old wives' tale? And are there other foods that might do the same thing? It's actually very hard to tell. However, one of the tips for remembering dreams is to break up your sleep pattern; therefore it makes sense that if certain foods are hard to digest, then this might contribute to a restless night, which in turn could help you to remember your dreams more. In addition to cheese, other foods that are difficult to digest include eels, currants, shellfish, cranberries, bananas, and pretty much all types of red meat.

In 2005, the Cheese Board in the UK carried out a pretty extensive experiment on the effects that cheese has on dreams. Two hundred volunteers took part in the study, in which they each ate .7 oz (20 g) of cheese half an hour before bedtime. According to the statistics, there were no reports of actual nightmares, but there were plenty of dreams recorded. This probably wasn't terribly surprising, but there were a couple of curveballs thrown into the cheesy equation. It seems that different varieties of cheese had different effects; eating Stilton Blue Cheese caused 85 per cent of the women to experience the freakiest dreams. Subject matter for these stiltonian dreams includes: talking toys; dinner party guests being traded for camels; and a vegetarian crocodile upset because it could not eat children.

Here at Freaky Dreams Central, we decided to conduct our own experiments into the effects of cheese on our dreams. Our experiment may not have been as far-reaching as that of the Cheese Board, but yielded interesting results nevertheless.

We asked six volunteers to eat as much cheese as they liked just before hopping into bed. We also asked six volunteers to deliberately avoid cheese on the same six days of the experiment.

THE RESULT?

Here's the shocker.

Cheese or no cheese seemed to make absolutely no difference whatsoever.
Some of the cheese-eaters had strange dreams; so, however, did the cheese-free volunteers. Here's one of the most coherent dream diaries that we received back from the volunteers. It's from Dan. He ate the cheese.

Night one: No dreams
Night two: Had a dream that I ate an enormous carton of fries, but the fries were in a big foil tray that was somehow floating in water inside a cardboard box, like a water bath, with Christmas gift wrap on. It looked a little bit like a Bain Marie or something.
Night three: I dreamt that I was in a London pub for New Year's Eve. Noel Gallagher was in there, and although he would talk to me he wouldn't let me have my picture taken with him. He kept moving around the table to prevent having his picture taken. His wife/girlfriend kept showing her stomach to people. I eventually had to leave in a hurry as I had spilt gravy all down my gray jumper.
Night four: No dreams
Night five: Had a dream I was at a vacation park on a lads' holiday for the weekend and got locked in the swimming pool overnight. It was quite lucid and I was quite anxious that I couldn't get out.
Night six: No dreams
Wow. Fries? Gravy? The Pub? Being locked in a swimming pool? Only Dan could analyze this dream with any certainty, but we'd say that it shows a level of fretfulness about his personal appearance while in the presence of a celebrity. This is quite understandable, but the slightly elusive nature of that celebrity might mean that Dan is frustrated about something. Anxiety about

being locked in a swimming pool, and the fries floating in the water bath, might imply a certain reluctance to integrate his feminine side, especially in such a masculine environment. That Dan is scarfing down large amounts of food tells us that he has a strong spiritual side that needs nurturing. And the lady showing her stomach to everyone is just plain freaky.

Another dream diary from a volunteer non-cheese eater came from Laura. Her journal shows some intriguing examples of dreams that involve her childhood and days gone by.

Night One: I'm riding a bike through my family vacation home, but the seat is far too high and I can't quite reach the peddles properly, wobbling all over the place. I think I'm leaving. I've got loads of bags that I'm struggling to carry, I keep dropping things and I can feel myself getting really frustrated and upset.

Night Two: My mum and I are searching around thrift stores looking for a skirt to wear for a fancy dress party, I'm going as a school girl. My surroundings change and I'm in another store, where I find hats which I begin to try on.

Night Three: No dreams

Night Four: I'm with family and my old dog, wandering around the garden where I grew up.

The river is in flood. We walk through some woods where there's a bees nest in the trunk of a big old tree. Next, we walk out of the woods and it's just me and my mum, we get in my car and start driving around a rotary, but I can't turn off, I don't know where I'm going.

Night Five: There are lots of people around, I'm in my underwear, but no-one seems to notice. I'm trying to find my apartment which is in a mall. I'm going up and down the escalators. There's also a spiral staircase. When I finally find my front door it's next to the amusements, I can see fruit machines and flashing lights. I realise that I've left my keys in the car, which is back down on the first floor parked among the stores. So I start going up and down the escalators again. Once again I can feel myself getting really frustrated and upset.

Night Six: No dreams.

Laura's dreams also involve some anxiety. She has the classic "underwear in public" aspect to a part of her dream, too—(*see* the section on nudity in dreams page 81). There's also a large degree of going back to her past; the old family home, the bicycle that's too big, and the time she spends in the dream with her mother might suggest that Laura is longing for a return to simpler days with fewer responsibilities.

Here are segments from more of the dreams that were reported back. We defy you to decide whether they were cheese-fuelled or not…here are some of the more coherent extracts.

I can't get into my house because the porch is covered with rabbits disguised as pineapples. They're wriggling all over the place and I don't want to step on them

I am standing inside a hamster wheel, having fun, then I realize it's not a hamster wheel but a gigantic roll of adhesive tape. Or am I just really tiny?

Aliens are going to invade the planet. They get here by climbing though radios that are set to a certain frequency. I am trying to stop people fiddling with their dials.

I look into my friend's pram to admire her new-born baby. There's no baby there, only a plate of dressed crab. But my friend seems pleased enough and I just can't tell her the truth.

I have a job interview and am hurrying to get ready. The only stuff in my wardrobe is full-sized animal skins, all evidently very recently skinned from the animals they belonged to because blood is dripping everywhere.

ANSWER; The first two dreams are cheese-fuelled. The last two are "normal."

"I was having a very deep and meaningful conversation with my cat, Mr. Bootsypuss, and then suddenly we were on the bed making out. I knew it was wrong, but it was fabulous sex. When I woke up and went to feed him in the morning, it was really weird. We've exchanged some meaningful stares since that night, and I wonder if he had the same dream."

COFFIN

The coffin is an example of a "container" dream (*See* **Bottle** *or* **Box**). The container, or in this case, coffin, represents you. The more obvious meaning of the coffin—death—can't be ignored, though. In this case, the coffin in your dream represents an ending of something, death making way for something new.

COLOR

Some people say that they never dream in color—or at least, if they do, then they don't notice what those colors are; it's likely that the colors are simply not significant within the dream. Sometimes, however, the colors in your dream cannot be ignored. Here's a guide to their (very) basic meanings:

Red = life, energy
Green = growth, harmony
Blue = spirituality, calmness
Pink = sexuality
Brown = earthiness
Yellow = childlike qualities
Black = mystery, decay
White = purity, cleanliness
Purple = magic and mystery

COMPASS

The main task of a compass is to indicate direction. In dreams, your subconscious mind communicates with you. Therefore, it's logical to suppose that dreaming of a compass means that your subconscious mind is trying to tell you something about the direction your life is taking. Perhaps you need to change it.

CONDOM

Condoms are protection. They protect us from STDs and stop women from getting pregnant. What, in your waking life, requires protection?
Your dream of condoms is a reminder that something needs to be looked after.

CONFETTI

It seems odd when you think about it that we like to have tiny scraps of paper flying through the air when we have something to celebrate. Confetti or tickertape in your dream means that you have something joyful to look forward to in real life.

CORRIDOR

A house or a building in a dream, represents you. A corridor is an area of transition, a path that leads us from one place to another—somewhere we don't generally linger. Perhaps there's such a transition taking place in your life at the moment, and you're in a metaphorical corridor between jobs, relationships, or homes.

CROWD

To find that you're in a crowd can either be upsetting and confusing or joyous and unifying—depending, of course, on the mood of the crowd. If the dream is a confusing crowd scene, then the feeling of trapped frustration might reflect a certain situation in your waking life. If the crowd is unified and joyful, then you might as well enjoy whatever is going on, knowing that you're one small but important component in a unified whole.

CUP

Any sort of a vessel, such as a cup, chalice, or goblet, represents the female aspect of your psyche. This applies whether you are male or female. If you are the former, this dream is telling you to follow your intuitions and your "feminine" side.

DAISY

Daisies stand for freshness, optimism, springtime, and new growth, as well as the innocence of childhood. Sometimes dreams remind us of what's missing in our lives, so the appearance of a daisy in your dream could be a gentle hint that perhaps things aren't that bad after all. New growth will come soon.

DANCING

If you were dancing by yourself, this dream implies that you can express yourself best when you're left alone. You might be feeling bogged down by the responsibilities of everyday waking life, but dancing alone in your dream shows that you're young inside, and the world is still your oyster. If you were dancing with a partner, this is an expression of harmony, both in your life and in your choice of sexual partner. Again, you might be fortunate in that this perfectly describes your situation, or it could be something you're craving.

DAUGHTER

If your daughter is a real person and you dream about her, the context of the dream will tell you if you're expressing your hopes for her or your anxieties about her. If you have no daughter, the girl in the dream represents a part of yourself. This is the case no matter whether you're male or female.

DEAD

There's a distinction between "dead" and "death," and so you'll find entries for both in this book. If someone that you know to be dead appears to you in a dream, there's a strong school of thought that would suggest the person is coming to you from the other side of the veil, so to speak, to impart information. There's an equally strong consideration that says our own subconscious mind will do whatever it can to get information passed to us, including disguising itself as a dead person. Either way, the message is likely to be an important one. Sometimes we dream that people close to us are dead. This is more likely to be a typical anxiety dream rather than a premonition dream.

If you dream of a dead animal, then the part of you that is represented by that animal might be dead for the time being. For example, if you dream of a dead bird, then perhaps you feel grounded, unable to "fly," metaphorically speaking.

DEAF

To dream that you are deaf, or that you are dealing with deaf people, means that you either can't get someone to hear what you are saying or that you are not listening to what someone is telling you. Pay attention, either way, and find a new way of communicating if necessary.

DEATH

Death signifies an end. If you dream that someone you know is dead, it's not necessarily a warning that you'll need to buy a black suit anytime soon. Rather, it might be that the useful parts of your relationship with this person have come to an end, and that it's time for you to acknowledge this.

If you dream that you yourself are dying, this is not an omen or an indication that you are near death. It means you're undergoing a profound

series of changes that will see you advance in every way imaginable. It's not nice seeing your body in a coffin, but if you do, see this as an exciting precursor to a whole new you!

DECAPITATION

What we're really talking about here is someone losing his or her head. If it's you, perhaps there is a decision you regret or an ill-advised choice that you've made that needs rectifying.

DEFORMITY

Essentially, a deformity is something that's wrong, something that's amiss. To dream of such a thing (be it a physical, emotional, or mental deformity) would imply that there's something similarly "wrong" with a situation in your life. A deformity doesn't necessarily have to be fixed; rather, we need to find ways to work with it or around it.

DÉJÀ VU

If you experience déjà vu during the course of your dream, this is a good indicator that your dream is about to go "lucid." (*See* **Lucid Dreaming** on page 156).

DEMONS

Carl Jung, one of the greatest influences on dream analysis, said that we each have a shadow side—a side that remains hidden. Devils, demons, and the like represent that shadow side, the aspects of ourselves that we might be ashamed of and that we prefer not to disclose to the world. It's also worth bearing in mind that we need to face our demons in order to understand them. Perhaps it's time to consider a little more integration and a little less distraction?

DENTIST

There's usually a degree of anxiety about seeing a dentist, even if we have a perfect set of gnashers. One of the most common anxiety dreams is about teeth falling out (*see* page 80), and a dentist dream also falls into the anxiety category.

DEVILS (*See* Demons)

DIAMONDS

Lovely! Generally speaking, it's good to dream of anything so beautiful and valuable. The diamond symbolizes strength, integrity, and clarity. So again, the context of the diamond is all. If you find a rough diamond, then there might be aspects of your character—or skills—that you feel are not being exploited. If you lose diamonds, then you're anxious about losing something of value in your waking life. Diamonds are, of course, given as a symbol of marriage, too, so this could also be a desire dream.

DINOSAUR

Possibly the most powerful symbol we have of outmoded ideas. Is there something you need to let go of?

DISGUISE

If in your dream you find yourself in a disguise, then you might not want people to know it's you. Try to remember your disguise as this could help you figure out what you're trying to hide, if anything. You have all these answers within you.

DISNEYLAND

Disneyland is something akin to a freaky dream itself. You may enjoy finding yourself in a fantasy full of pastel-colored castles and ten-foot high mice, or you may find the whole thing a surreal nightmare. Either way, the dream is an indication that it's time for you to embrace a new way of looking at things, to unexpect the expected, and to let your inner child come out to play.

DOCTOR

This is a guidance dream. As with any dream featuring a figure of authority, the doctor signifies the need for expert, trusted advice. It's most likely that your subconscious mind throws you in to visit a medical doctor, but it could be another kind. The issue you're facing need not be medical at all, but it does indicate that you need advice in an area of your life. The context of the dream will help you determine the type of advice needed.

DOG

Man's best friend packs a very powerful symbolic punch when he appears in a dream. We've always imposed important significance on these creatures; for example, in many societies they're considered to be "psycho—pomps," that is, animals that escort human souls to the next world. A black dog is thought to be a symbol of depression. Your dream doggie could also represent faithfulness, generosity, loyalty, and protection. It's important to recognize the context in which the dog appears in your dream. It might be barking at you as though it wants to tell you something. It might bite you, which would suggest that you need to pay attention to something. You might find that the dog appears to be guiding you somewhere; this is a strong signal for you to follow your intuition.

DONKEY

What's the word you most associate with this animal? Stubborn, perhaps? If you feel the animal is an aspect of yourself, then maybe you're being a bit stuck in your ways. The donkey could

also represent a situation that's been frustrating you. If, however, you're leading the donkey in the dream, then you've got a tricky situation under control.

DONUTS

Tasty, delicious, and fattening donuts speak of illicit desires—in particular, sexual ones.

DOVE

The world over, this little bird is symbolic of peace, harmony, contentment, gentility, and fertility. The white dove signifies spirituality.

DRESS (See Clothing)

DROWNING

Drowning dreams frequently end as the sleeper wakes suddenly; the feeling of panic unbearable. Being submerged in water and unable to breathe is a horrible feeling, and to dream of this is a powerful way for your subconscious mind to rap sharply against the door of your conscious mind, telling you to express your fears and anxieties in your everyday life. One dream might be enough for you, but if you dream repeatedly that you're drowning, then it might be worth seeking professional advice about confronting your fears.

DRUMMING

If you're drumming in the dream, then you're in control of your life. If you have to follow someone else's rhythm, however, then the opposite is true. You might be happy with this state of affairs, or you may not. What you do about it is up to you.

DYNAMITE

A good friend and a devastating enemy, dynamite represents very powerful aspects of yourself that you feel might endanger you in some way. The most powerful tool we have as human beings is that of speech. Words can be used like dynamite, equally explosive. Is there something you'd like to say that you've been sitting on for a while? Are you afraid of the consequences? Sometimes an explosion can clear the air, so long as you take care not to get hit by shrapnel.

EAGLE

One of the most prominent bird symbols, an eagle appearing in your dream speaks of glory, grandeur, royalty, authority—and immense power. The word "acumen," meaning keen-sightedness, shares its root with the Latin word for eagle, *aquila*.

Eagles soar high and can see things at great distances—and while you're dreaming, the skill of far-sightedness can also be used in relation to events in your life. Because of its power, the context in which the eagle appears in your dream is similarly amplified. If you're soaring with the birds or feel that you are the bird, this is a very good omen because of the bird's power and far-sightedness. On the other hand, if you see eagles chained up or confined in any way, then your dream is relating an incredibly frustrating experience that you are currently experiencing in your life. The bird's confinement parallels your own frustrations. If you kill an eagle in your dream, then this has two potential meanings. The first is that you believe you are more powerful and ruthless than an eagle. The second is that you are somehow destroying the most important and powerful aspect of yourself in your waking life. Take care.

EARS

If ears figure prominently in your dream, particularly ones with earrings, this is a nudge that you're not listening properly. The earrings draw more attention to the ears and so "amplify" their meaning.

EARTHQUAKE

Earthquake dreams have a clear meaning; there's a huge shake-up going on in your life, the outcome of which is still unpredictable. If you're rescuing people from the fissures in the earth, you're in charge of this shaky situation. You'll soon overcome any challenges that occur as the result of your changing circumstances. If you're not doing anything during the earthquake dream, then it indicates that you believe the situation's outcome is out of your control.

EGGS

Fertility, birth, new beginnings, and potential; this is what the humble egg stands for. A nest egg (a nest full of eggs) also indicates financial security. If the egg is broken deliberately, then you're happily in charge of your life. If the egg breaks by accident, however, events and situations in your life might be heading in the wrong direction. Scrambled eggs speak of confusion and misunderstandings.

ELECTRIC CHAIR

Not nice. An electric chair could indicate that you're feeling under threat from a particular person or institution.

ELEPHANT

We associate elephants with longevity and memory. Generally, they move slowly because of their cumbersome size, but if they need to, they can run like hell.

If you dream of an elephant, the context of the dream will indicate which elephant association carries the most important message from your subconscious. Has something from the past cropped up that you need to forget about again? Is there a large and cumbersome problem standing in your way? A white elephant indicates there is an unwanted element in your life. Because of their longevity and their powerful memories, elephants are believed to be wise. If you are an elephant in your dream, or are riding one, then you share its powers of wisdom.

E-MAIL

Oh dear! This is quite a feature of modern dreamers. If you dream of e-mails, then you either need to communicate something or you've been spending too much time in front of a computer screen.

EMERALD

Green is the color of growth and healing, and the emerald is one of the most precious gems. Therefore, to dream of emeralds is very auspicious. You could be experiencing growth in a particular area of your life, and emeralds could also indicate you have nascent healing powers.

ENGAGEMENT

If you dream that you're happily engaged, this could speak of your desire to "belong" to someone else, and you might want to question why this is, especially if there's no significant relationship in your life. If the dream engagement makes you nervous, on the other hand, you have to ask yourself why. Maybe there's a very good opportunity staring you in the face that you're reluctant to accept for some reason? It could also indicate that you're commitment-phobic, not necessarily about getting married, but about a potential new job, for example?

ENTRAILS

Entrails, at one time, were an important means of predicting the future. The efficacy of such a method would presumably depend upon the owner of the entrails. If the entrails in the dream belong to you, then the future outcome is unlikely to be fabulous. If you dream that you are handling entrails, then you're getting into the heart of an important issue in your waking life.

ENVELOPE

An unopened envelope signifies an exciting opportunity. If the envelope is red, then it's particularly good news.

EROTIC DREAMS

Erotic imagery in your dreams usually indicates a lack of sexual excitement in your real life. If this is the case, you have two choices. Either get out more, or sleep more, hoping that more of those saucy dreams will come your way.

EVERGREENS

This is a good dream to have if the evergreens are healthy. It indicates prosperity, security, and youthful qualities for you. If the evergreens are being chopped down, however, you might be anxious about something you've not yet discussed with anyone.

EVIL

Sometimes, certain dreams have a palpable feeling of evil attached to a particular person, place, or situation. If you've experienced it in a dream, then you know it. Some schools of thought believe that this is genuine evil, sneaking into your dream, and that you should protect yourself before you fall asleep. Others will tell you that the evil feeling exposes your own true feelings about the person, place, or situation in the dream, and that it's nothing to worry about. It's up to you to decide which you believe.

EXAMINATION

Taking an examination or test is a very common dream—so common, in fact, that it's one of the most popular dreams out there. (*See* page 83 for a full analysis of this dream.) If you dream, however, that you are closely examining the internal workings of anything—a human being, a machine, plants—then you need to take a closer look at something in your waking life. This is a call to action.

EXCAVATION

Digging in the earth is a dream metaphor for trying to understand ourselves better. Usually, we excavate in order to find treasure of some description, or to equip ourselves with information and knowledge about how people lived in the past. Such a process is painstaking and careful, but usually worth it since we're looking into our own past. The dream is encouraging you to try to find your own inner treasures so that they can be brought into the daylight as well as into the future.

DIGITAL DREAMS

I dreamed that I was in a room full of computers. They were all different kinds, one of those huge ones that was the size of a truck, and also some tiny little ones the size of phones with tiny screens that could project the information onto walls. (I do think that this would be a genius idea!)

You could tell the computers what to do simply by talking to them, and they answered in proper human voices, and it was important to choose the right one because it would become your special friend. The problem for me in the dream was trying to decide which one would be "mine." I didn't want to say anything in case I offended any of the computers, and then I woke up.

- Alicia

It is astonishing just how quickly human beings can embrace new technology. Children, for example, seem to be born with an innate ability to understand the labyrinthine workings of the latest cell phones, laptops, and MP3's without resorting to any boring instruction manuals. It's almost instinctive, as though such information is available to that generation alone.

Probably the most prevalent use of the computer, the one that will define our generation for sure, is its capability for communication, whatever form that might take: email, text messaging, blogging, Bluetooth connectivity, or all the many and varied platforms for social networking. We already know that an object in a dream essentially symbolizes itself, and although computers have been around for a while they are new enough for their symbolic meanings to have remained clear and true.

The computer, as a communicative tool, symbolizes both expansion and contraction; they make the world a bigger place by being able to measure, and count, and place in order, and yet, they make it smaller, by showing links and connections that no other "tool" has the speed or capability to demonstrate in the same efficient way.

To dream of digital objects, like a computer, is to realize your own capacity for expansion, too. This expansion surprisingly has a deep spiritual aspect, since the computer has the ability to link like-minded people based on a matrix of similarities. Some people have also gone so far as to draw parallels between the computer and God, and therefore the nearly religious aspects of computer-based communication and dreams cannot be ignored.

Digital dreams also throw up questions as to the nature of God. Computers are man-made, and yet, they have God-like qualities. Does this mean that there are also aspects of God that we might have "invented?"

In the dream sequence from Alicia on the opposite page, she seems to be almost afraid of the computer; she doesn't want to make the wrong choice lest she "offends." In this capacity, she is according computers, with human/godlike qualities. She also has a brainwave about the possibility of how computers could operate. This indicates both an understanding of what she's dealing with, but also, a modicum of fear too.

EXHIBITION

If this is a typical art-gallery exhibition in your dream, then it represents a fabulous opportunity for self-understanding and exploration. Dream analysts say that each picture or piece of art in the exhibition represents an aspect of you and your personality. If you love what you see and admire the fine brushwork and sensitive approach to the subject matter, then all is well and you are happy with yourself. If you find yourself in a gallery full of pictures that are repulsive to you (painted with gorilla excrement, perhaps?), then you are unhappy with aspects of yourself and should consider what these aspects are and how to change them.

EXPLORATION

Dreaming of any kind of exploration, whether you're sporting a colonial throwback or not, likely means that you are considering getting to know the uncharted territory of yourself better. This is one of the most exciting times that you will ever encounter in your life, and it might manifest in many different ways: a form of artistic expression, meditation, yoga, writing, the study of philosophy, or whatever. Oh and, of course, dream analysis. Enjoy yourself and happy hunting.

EXPLOSION

If there's an explosion in your dream, it's likely that you wake up panicked. If you go straight back to sleep, then you might be lucky enough to "climb back into" the dream *(see* **Lucid Dreaming** on page 156) and find out what the causes were. In general, an explosion is the end result of something that has been trapped for far too long and has nowhere else to go. Psychically speaking, the portents of such a dream can only be good for you. Once the dust has settled and the destruction dealt with, you will have a fresh new chapter in your life.

EXTRA SENSORY PERCEPTION (ESP)

If you dream that you're psychic and can read people's thoughts, then there is something important to consider. The dream could be telling you that you need to understand people a little better, show more empathy, and try to see their point of view.

EYES

The appearance of eyes—the windows of the soul—in your dream is all a matter of context. If there are many eyes staring at you, then you're under unfair scrutiny in your waking life. If the eyes appear as well-known symbols, such as the eye on top of the pyramid on the dollar bill or the eyes of the Buddha that appear on the designs of temples, then there is a higher vision going on within you. Pay attention to what else is going on in this dream.

If you have something stuck in your eye, this indicates that you're not seeing something properly and you should remove whatever is psychologically blocking you. If you realize that you have a third eye in your dream, then you're coming into a time of profound spiritual awakening.

FACEBOOK

It's incredible just how quickly Facebook has become a household word and a common part of our cultural currency. I'm reluctant to state here just how many members this social networking site has around the planet, since the figure will have probably quadrupled by the time I finish writing it.

Anything so iconographic is naturally subject matter for a dream, but in order to analyze what a Facebook dream means, we have to get to the core of what Facebook is about. It's about communication and sharing information, with no boundaries beyond access to a computer. Therefore, your own communication skills are reflected in the dream; perhaps you need to alter your methods of communication, maybe find new ways of searching for information or different ways to interact with friends. Look at the areas of your life that are concerned with communication and see what lessons can be drawn from your dream. It's also possible that you might be relying on Facebook a little too much; there's nothing like a direct face-to-face chat.

FACTORY

Factory work is often associated with mind-numbing repetition, so dreaming of a factory would suggest that you may be facing a similar situation in your real life; maybe not quite so bad, but nevertheless a situation of boredom and tedium that you should look at with a view to changing.

FAIRGROUND

Fairgrounds are colorful, wonderful, noisy, and lively places—but they can also have a sinister feel. In dreams, a fairground often signifies childhood. Children can often be frightened of things that seem perfectly normal to the adult eye. Their febrile young imaginations see faces where there are no faces, and the toys and characters in a fairground can seem scarily real. To dream of a fairground can be to dream of fears hidden since childhood. Your own feeling during such a dream will tell you whether or not this is the case.

FAIRY

A fairy appearing in a dream might represent a hidden aspect of you. Two things that all fairies have in common are magical powers and the ability to fly; think of Tinkerbell, for example. Fairies, too, are unpredictable and have values that humans might find rather suspect. Perhaps there is a moral conflict in your life that you've been struggling with? The fairy in your dream is a reminder that these qualities are present in your own life. A fairy dream could also be a yearning to return to the innocent days of your childhood, a time when a belief in fairies and other fantastical creatures was accepted as "normal."

FALLING

To dream that you're falling is a very common anxiety dream. (*See* page 84 for a full analysis and an in-depth look.)

FAMILY

Analysis of what it means if you see your family in a dream depends entirely on your relationship with them. If you get along well with them, you might be anticipating a happy get-together, perhaps to celebrate a significant anniversary. If, on the other hand, relationships are less than cordial, then dreaming of your family is more likely to indicate anxieties in your life. There is probably something in your life that you have to do that you'd much rather not, such as undertaking a duty that's not exactly thrilling for you.

FANGS

Vampires are big news right now, so it stands to reason that some of you may be experiencing an increased volume of fang-featured fantasies in your dreams. Despite the horror of having your neck bitten into by a vampire and all the ensuing consequences, there are also strong sexual overtones here, too, which are a powerful underlying theme of vampire tales. Dreaming of fangs could be a case of repressed sexual desire on your part.

THE AWARD FOR "MOST POPULAR DREAM" GOES TO...

The most common dreams fall into six categories. The first five are all anxiety dreams, but the sixth is a lot more pleasant. In no particular order, these are:

1. YOUR TEETH ARE FALLING OUT
2. YOU'RE NAKED IN A PLACE THAT YOU SHOULDN'T BE NAKED
3. YOU'RE BEING CHASED—OFTEN BY A NON-HUMAN ENTITY
4. YOU'RE TAKING AN EXAM, AND YOU'RE COMPLETELY UNPREPARED FOR IT (EVEN IF IT'S BEEN YEARS SINCE YOU'VE BEEN IN SCHOOL)
5. YOU'RE FALLLLING...!
6. YOU'RE FLYIIIING...!

"ARGGGGH...MY TEETH ARE FALLING OUT!"

This wasn't really a dream but a nightmare, and I've never forgotten it. I'm getting dolled up to go to a party or something, and I can see myself very clearly in a mirror—this is the only time I've ever actually seen myself in a dream. I'm looking great, good hair, lovely makeup. I smile at myself, and my teeth sort of fall out of my mouth, all black and rotten, and I can even taste the blood in my mouth. I screamed in my dream and woke myself up, thank God.
-Julie

Have you ever had one of those awful dreams in which your teeth are falling out? Sometimes they might be wobbling freely, or they might just crumble to dust at the slightest touch. It's a hideous feeling, and it's weird how the feeling of anxiety and horror can stick with you for quite some time.

Our teeth say an awful lot about us these days. As a society, we can spend fortunes on whitening them, straightening them or altering the odd little snaggle tooth. Retainers, once seen worn only by school children, are now a regular sight in grown adults. Teeth have become an important status symbol in recent years, and this new aspect of our gnashers only serves to increase the anxiety we feel when we lose them, even if it is only in the dream and not in real life.

Teeth aren't just a status symbol. Although dentures are common, teeth—real or fake—are a vital piece of our survival equipment, used to break down food into acceptable chunks for digestion. They're also a powerful symbol of sexuality; would you really want to kiss someone with a mouthful of rotten teeth?

Therefore it's quite right to suppose that to dream of losing your teeth is an anxiety dream *par excellence*. It's up to you to discover exactly what these anxieties are, and to find ways of allaying them. When you have a dream about losing your teeth, reflect on what happened earlier in the day so a pattern emerges. Things are never usually as bad as you might think, and it often helps just to talk things through with a neutral party.

"OH NO...I'M NOT WEARING ANY CLOTHES!"

It's the same dream every time, and it has its roots in a real-life incident. I'm wandering around in a hotel room with no clothes on. I open the closet door, but behind it is a ballroom full of people I don't know, and I'm standing, stark naked, in front of all of them. They're all laughing. It's excruciating. The real-life incident happened when I was a pre-teen, also naked in a hotel room, the door opened and a family of people walked in with the porter, who had taken them to the wrong room.
-Jeff

Nearly everyone has had a naked dream experience at least once. At first, everything seems entirely normal. You're going about your everyday business. You may be on a bus, a train, or in a store...then you suddenly realize that you're absolutely stark naked. OOPS. And you don't know what you can do to hide your embarrassment. It's also common to find that no one else in the dream notices your clothes-free status, or at least, if they do, they don't make a point of commenting on it. This is a moot point, however, as we shall see below.

Ever since Eve handed Adam the fig leaf, thereby drawing attention to the fact that he was slightly superior to the animals and therefore needed to protect his modesty, we have worn clothes. For thousands of years, we've concealed our nakedness with all manner of skins, beads, feathers, and fabrics. Therefore, regardless of your general attitude toward nudity, if you find yourself naked in a public place in which it's inappropriate or even illegal, it's a serious taboo. So what does this mean in a dream?

We need to think very clearly about what clothes are and what they do. Effectively, they conceal our real state. They also allow us to give an impression of ourselves; clothes send out a clear statement to the world about who we are and what we do. Nurse. Businessman. Hippy. Rockstar. Policeman.

As well as revealing our identity, clothes are also a very efficient way of masking it, too. In short, they can be a disguise, if we wish them to be.

Therefore when we have a "naked" dream, we are having an anxiety dream that our identity is being taken away; that we are vulnerable and unprotected. There is also the possibility that, in real life, you're trying to hide something, but a part of you feels that you're going to get caught out. Do you feel like you're "getting away" with certain aspects of your life—maybe you feel under qualified to be doing your job? Underlying insecurities of all kinds can result in "naked" dreams.

"HELP! SOMETHING'S CHASING ME!"

I'm running and running, never sure what from, but the run ends when I have to jump off the edge of something; sometimes it's a cliff, sometimes a tall building, one time it was even a bridge of some kind. As soon as I jump, I wake up with a start.

-Anna

What do you do if you're in real danger? Most of us would probably try to get away from that danger as fast as possible. Thankfully it's unlikely that most of us will be chased by a bear, tiger, or mad axeman in real life. Well, in a dream, our response is usually the same—to run away.

Dreams elicit primitive responses from our subconscious minds, and running away from a stressful situation is a pretty logical thing to do. Indeed it's almost a shame that we can't just get the hell out when life's stresses get to be too much. Instead, in real life, we have to confront the metaphorical wild animals and mad axemen that chase us in the dream.

There's another aspect to the "chasing" dream however. Besides running away from our daily stresses, there's a distinct possibility that the thing we're running away from is an aspect of ourselves, something that we're afraid of facing. This could be anger, jealousy, a fear of failure—or even of success. You might even be running away from your own powers, strengths, and talents, afraid of the inherent responsibilities that they might bring with them.

"OH NO! I'VE GOT A TEST, AND I'M TOTALLY UNPREPARED FOR IT!"

Yes, the exams dream. I still sometimes have those dreams where I'm about to take an exam, and it really takes me back to high school. I quite enjoy these dreams now, because when I wake up I'm so thankful that it's not real anymore!

- Harry

Who hasn't experienced this sort of dream at one time or another? It's hideous. There you are, mature, experienced, probably well-established with a professional career and a family. Then *whoomf!* You're suddenly plunged back into the dreaded days of school or college with an exam looming which you're certain you are about to fail.

But don't fret unduly. This sort of a dream usually means that you're putting yourself under pressure, and there's really nothing to worry about. The residual feeling of anxiety, though, should be addressed. The feeling of being unprepared might be real, but the feeling of dread will only make things worse.

It might also be that there's someone in your waking life—likely in your workplace—that is making you feel as though you are being judged against others. Sometimes, just recognizing the cause of an anxiety can be enough to dispel it.

"AAAAARGH...I'M FALLING!"

I used to have falling dreams a lot when I was a kid, so much so that my folks took me to see a shrink. The best one ever, though, was when I sort of switched the falling sensation around in my dream, and made it so I was flying instead. The falling dreams seemed to stop soon after that so I assume I'd made some kind of mental progress.
-Jennifer

Have you ever had one of those dreams where you're falling? The plummet often ends with you being jolted awake, back into consciousness, with your arms still flailing trying to grab hold of something. Such a feeling is all too real and can leave you with a residual shakiness—although you usually fall asleep again pretty quickly.

It's commonly believed that these types of dreams reflect inner turmoil and anxieties. You could be worried, metaphorically speaking, about losing your "foothold" in a certain situation, or of losing your balance or equanimity. Or you might have taken on too much responsibility.

However, a falling dream can also happen for entirely different reasons. They're usually experienced at the beginning of a sleep pattern and can be caused by a natural drop in blood pressure. They can also be the result of another type of natural reaction called a "myclonic jump" or "jerk." This is an involuntary muscle spasm and usually nothing to worry about, although if you start to experience such reactions more frequently, or when you're awake, you might want to seek medical advice.

"WHEEEE...I'M FLYING!"

I always dream I can fly. It seems so easy. You just step up into the air, one foot after another. And once I'm in the air, I can soar for hours. I wonder why I don't know how to do this when I'm awake. It's so blindingly obvious!
-Theo

This is the only "popular" dream that has nothing to do with anxiety. But there are two types of flying dreams. One is a "normal" dream. If you're soaring above rooftops, this is great. It implies confidence in yourself and satisfaction with your life. You've got perspective, you can see the bigger picture, and for all intents and purposes, you're at the top of your game.

The second type of flying dream is often a result of, or precursor to, a lucid dream. A lucid dream (*see* page 156) is where a high level of consciousness creeps into your sleep, enabling you to "control" your dream events. If you're having a lucid dream where you're flying, don't suddenly question what you're doing; if you do, you might suddenly find that you're falling, and this requires swift conscious thought to set things right before you wake up.

If mastered properly, the flying dream will not only give you hours of dreamtime enjoyment, but you might also find that your self-confidence improves in your waking life.

FARM

Anything to do with agriculture, farming, or animal welfare speaks of maturity, responsibility, and sensibility. Your dream is telling you that you need to work hard to achieve worthwhile and long-lasting results. You've either begun doing this or you know that you should.

FATHER

Regardless of whether your father has passed away or is still alive, and regardless of your actual relationship with him, the father figure that appears in your dream is more than the sum of his parts, since he appears as the paternal archetype. But what does this mean?

As the paternal archetype, the father stands for security, protection, paternal authority, and affection. The flipside of all these qualities includes tyranny, restrictions, and aggression. We can draw upon all these different aspects of the father figure, and know where they are coming from. So that you can have a greater understanding of what your father means if he appears to you in a dream, you need to remember the context of the dream. You may be overjoyed to see him, in which case you've embraced all those fatherly qualities; you might be afraid of him, which means that you're equally afraid of the responsibilities that come with paternal authority, or the situation might seem quite normal. His appearance means that there are aspects of paternal characteristics that you need to be able to understand and absorb to become a more fully rounded person. It's also important to remember that the father is an authority figure, so you should listen carefully to his words if he speaks in your dream. It could be a guidance dream.

FEATHER

Because they come from the wings of birds—and, in dreamland, from the wings of angels—feathers are a happy dream omen and tend to bring with them information of some kind, or a comforting reminder of something or someone.

FEET

The foundation and balancing point of the body, the feet, in a dream, symbolize similar ideals. So if you see your feet or someone else's, then it's likely that you or the foot owner are solid, secure, and well balanced. The feet, after all, are in pretty much constant contact with the earth! However, if you see only one foot, then that balance in your life has been skewed for some reason.

FENCE

The fence signifies a boundary between places. To be "on the fence" about something implies a boundary between opinions or ideas. A fence is also a barrier, providing protection (think of the word "defense"). If you're constructing a fence in your dream, it's possible that you're feeling the need to protect or defend yourself in your waking life.

FIG

Figs are symbols of eroticism and fertility, so if one turns up in a dream, unexpected pleasure could await you. Alternately, if you're trying to get pregnant, figs are a good omen.

FIG LEAF

Some symbols occupy a very powerful place in our subconscious because of generations of association. For more than 2,000 years, we've been told that fig leaves were used by Adam and Eve to preserve their modesty when they suddenly realized that they were naked. Therefore, we see the fig leaf as a symbol not only as the loss of innocence, but as one of modesty and the preservation of embarrassment. If you're wearing a fig leaf in your dream, like those biblical characters, then events in your life are making you feel the need to protect yourself somehow.

FINGERNAILS

These can indicate a lot about our sense of self-esteem. If your dream fingernails are in good condition, trimmed and healthy, then you have good self-esteem and a positive outlook on your life. If they are bitten or broken in the dream, then you could be feeling below par and/or anxious about something. Broken nails also indicate low self esteem. Nails with bright red polish hint at your erotic side.

FIRE

Fire is beautiful powerful, dangerous, illuminating, destructive, or purifying. And so its meaning depends entirely on how the fire presents itself in your dream. If it's a fire that you can't control, then maybe there's a similarly heated and uncontrollable situation in your own life—think about the flames fanned by desire. If you are put in the situation of controlling the fire and you do this successfully, then the dream is showing you that you're more powerful than you had thought. If you are burned by the fire, then you might be getting involved in something in your waking life that may similarly result in you getting "burned."

FISH

Like birds, fish can carry messages for us in dreams, so look out for potential messages there. Water represents the female element and fish can mean new life, so it's not surprising that some women dream of swimming fish even before they know that they are pregnant. Fish also symbolize emotions; you may have deep-seated feelings that you're finding difficult to express. Try to let them come to the surface in your waking life. If you dream that you're fishing, then it's likely that you have started to make conscious attempts to get these feelings to the surface—you're not afraid to deal with them anymore.

FISSURE (See Cave)

FLYING

Flying is a very common dream, and a full detailed analysis can be found on page 85.

FLOATING

Not as common as flying, floating is still borne of the same feeling of relaxation and letting go. Floating dreams indicate that you're extremely comfortable with who you are and where you are in your life. Sometimes you can induce a floating dream using lucid dream techniques (*see* page 156).

FLOOD

Since water is often representative of emotions, dreaming of a flood symbolizes the sudden bursting forth of emotions, to the point where real damage can take place. If in the dream you are caught up in the deluge, then you need to realize that there's a possibility that this might happen in your waking life—metaphorically speaking, naturally. The dream is a warning to be aware of this and deal with a situation before it's too late.

FLOWERS

Depending on the condition of the flowers, this can be a good dream or not. Bright, healthy, colorful flowers tell you that you have a happy soul. The opposite—drooping, dying, or desiccated flowers are not so good. If you're given beautiful flowers in a dream, some people believe that this is a gift from the spirit realms, especially if they're accompanied by a friend or relative that has gone over to the "other side." If you see flowers blooming in impossible conditions, then unexpected good news is coming your way soon. Among the most popular flowers, the red rose stands for love, so hopefully your dream reflects your real-life situation, whereas the lily is a reminder of death, not necessarily of a person, but of a situation, friendship, job, etc.

FLIES

If you have flies buzzing around in your dream, this indicates that there are aspects of your life that you feel are unclean or out of control.

FOOD

Food symbolizes the material body as well as the emotional state, and the quantity, type, and quality of the food speaks volumes. If you find yourself eating something you never normally touch—for example, if you're a vegetarian and you find yourself eating meat in a dream—this isn't a sign that you should suddenly swap your lentils for lamb chops, but an indication that you should try something new in your life. If you're stuffing chocolates into your mouth while ignoring a table full of more sustaining fare, then there is an imbalance somewhere in your waking life; an area that has been neglected and needs to be fulfilled.

FORGETFULNESS

Sometimes in dreams we forget where we are; familiar places become unfamiliar, locations change, things become misplaced. We could go into a long analysis of why this is, but it comes down to that same old chestnut: anxiety.

FOUNTAIN

Fountains can have phallic connotations and signify repressed desires. However, the fountain is also symbolic of happiness and joy. Only the context of the fountain in your dream and an insightful look into your own life will let you know which it's to be.

FOX

Foxes are smart, cunning, and clever enough to outwit the hounds that pursue them. Yes, the fox is ultimately adaptable and if you follow the tip that you have access to all the qualities of the animals you dream about, then rest assured that to dream about the fox is very handy indeed. If a person that you know appears as a fox in a dream, then this might be a warning not to trust the person because of their cunning, sly, foxlike qualities.

FRAME

A frame is usually square and defines a boundary, so it can be viewed as a sort of cage since it effectively "traps" its subject within its boundaries. That's why it's important to observe what's in the frame in your dream. Whatever is displayed in the frame is something that you wish to remain intact or unchanging. A family portrait or wedding photo, perhaps? If the frame in your dream is empty, then you're waiting for someone to fill it.

FROG

Living somewhere between the earth and the water and with a very visible life cycle, the frog—for all its comic value—is a magical creature of transformation, and that's what is signifies your dream. Remember the frog that turned into a prince after a kiss from the princess? You, too, or something in your life, is undergoing or will undergo a major transformation.

FUNERAL

Signifying an end and a "saying goodbye," to dream of attending your own funeral is more common than you might suppose. Don't worry, you're not going to be sitting on a cloud playing a harp any time soon, but there will be an opportunity to say goodbye to an aspect of yourself that has passed its sell-by date. If you're burying a friend, then the same point is true; you won't necessarily lose the friend, just an outdated aspect of the relationship. Similarly, if you dream of a parental funeral and the parent is still alive, then it's time to cut free from parental constraints and influences.

FURNITURE

Another relatively popular dream is that you're moving furniture around in a house. Both house and furniture may or may not be familiar. Remember that the house represents you, and the furniture symbolizes aspects of your character. Rearranging this "soul" furniture means that there are things about yourself that you would similarly like to alter.

"I'm downstairs in my friend's house. It looks the same, but it's different. The window is different. It is nighttime and I open the window, which is long with the hinge that opens it along the top. There's a steep road right outside the window, and hundreds of ghostly white horses are coming down the road. They come to the open window and put their heads through into the room and look at me. I know that they want to tell me something very important—a secret."

GALLOWS

A gloomy dream to have. Criminals were once hanged from the gallows as a form of execution, and their appearance in a dream is an indication that something in your life is about to come to an end. This could be a relationship or a job, for example. Because the gallows are about "hanging," it's possible that whatever it is that's going to end is long overdue.

GARAGE

Garages are transitional places, not somewhere you'd necessarily want to spend a long time, but closely associated with vehicles and therefore with travel. To dream of a garage could indicate that you're waiting for something to happen or that travel or a vacation is in your future.

GARBAGE

Garbage only becomes garbage because we no longer have a use for it. Similarly, garbage in a dream represents ideas, relationships, and situations that have passed their sell-by date and that need to be cleared away.

GARDEN (GARDENING)

Broadly speaking, the garden—and gardening—represents your spiritual side and the nurturing of it. Accordingly, if everything is rosy in the garden, then all is well. But if the garden is unkempt and disheveled, then your subconscious mind is telling you, metaphorically, to get out there and do some weeding.

GARLAND

The shape suggests wholeness and completion, a never-ending circle, the same as the wedding ring. If you are garlanded or being crowned with flowers, then perhaps your dreams are giving you the praise that you feel you're not receiving in your waking life. (*See* **Wreath** on page 276.)

GARLIC

If you dream that you're eating garlic, then this could indicate that you feel that you need to protect yourself from something in your waking life.

GAS MASK

If you dream that you're wearing a gas mask, it's likely that you feel the need to filter out an unhealthy influence in your life; this is unlikely to be a noxious substance, but more likely a person or situation that's just not very edifying. The dream is telling you to tackle whatever it is that's causing the anxiety in the first place.

GATE, GATEWAY

In Japan, there's a sacred gateway called a *torii* that marks the boundary between a secular space and a sacred space. This is the perfect expression of the primal idea that a gate or a gateway marks a definition between two states of being. This idea isn't something that you'd necessarily think of in your normal waking life, but one that is known by your subconscious mind. If you are stepping through a gateway in your dream, then a transition of some kind is occurring in your life. Although the gate is a luminal, threshold place, the transition is swift; it's not like a bridge, where the process is slower and more gradual. Bear in mind that the two "states of being" separated by the gateway can include geographical states as well as spiritual and psychic ones.

GAY (*See* Homosexuality)

GEMSTONES

Chances are that if you dream of gemstones, then you'll be pretty certain that you dreamed of them in color. The jewels in your dream are a reminder of the treasures in your waking life. This doesn't mean that you're suddenly going to see a significance increase in your bank balance—riches are not just about money. After all, gemstones are taken from the ground and only ascribed a value by the people that want them. Some of the most precious gems are the things in your life that are, effectively, free, so think about who or what the gemstones are representing in your life.

GHOSTS

If you dream of a ghost, then try to remember the feeling that you had when you encountered the dream apparition. Some people believe that if the spirit of a deceased person appears to you in a dream, then it's likely that the actual ghost is really trying to make contact with you. Or it could be that you feel something was left unresolved in the relationship.

If you dream that you yourself are the ghost, then this could indicate that you are somewhat disenfranchised from your own life; that people don't hear what you are saying or take no notice of you. If you feel like a ghost in your dream, you need to find ways to come back to life, metaphorically speaking, when you're awake. If someone you know appears as a ghost in your dream, this could be an instance of your friend doing some astral traveling into your sleep space...or it could be an anxiety dream related to death and loss.

GIFTS

If you receive a gift in your dream, the gift itself is likely to be a metaphor, a symbol of something else. It could be something that you have forgotten that you already have that the dream is reminding you of. Or it could be something that you need in your life. If, on the other hand, you are giving a gift to someone else, remember that you can only give something that you have already, and that giving is closely aligned to sharing. Once again, the gift you are giving will be symbolic of something else, and only you will be able to interpret what the object actually signifies.

GLOBE

If you see a model globe of the Earth in your dream, this means that you are or likely will be planning a long trip.

GLOVES

Are you wearing gloves in your dream, or do they feature prominently? We generally wear gloves if we want to protect our hands from something. If you are the one wearing the gloves in the dream, then you are trying to keep a secret or hide something. If someone else is wearing the gloves, then they are hiding something from you.

GOAL

Whether or not you're a soccer aficionado, the dream of scoring a goal with the crowd going crazy is probably not one you want to wake up from too soon. If you have this dream, it implies that you've been striving for something very difficult, but it's not unobtainable. Keep working at it!

GOAT

Goats are determined, hardy, adaptable, and are, of course, the totem animal of people born under the astrological sign of Capricorn. Perhaps the goat is a reminder of someone in your life with these qualities? Goats are also symbols of sexuality and lechery. So if, for example, you're afraid of the goat in your dream, then perhaps you're scared of expressing your sexual desires.

GOD

Within 24 hours of seeing the god, Jupiter, in his dream, Caligula was efficiently assassinated and presumably got to meet Him in person (*see* page 132 for more details about **Prophecies of Doom**). If you find that God is talking to you in a dream, it's unlikely that you will suffer the same fate, but it's important to pay attention to whatever He (or She) is telling you. Which brings us to another point; how does the deity appear in your dream? Is it the bearded old gent of the Judeo-Christian persuasion? Although many of us eschew this image, it is iconic, and instantly recognizable and therefore good material for your subconscious. If your God appears in the form of a woman, then part of what She is telling you is that anything is possible, and to unexpect the expected in your waking life.

GOLD

Consider the alchemist. We have an idea that his or her quest was to turn base metal (lead) into a very valuable one (gold). However, the real alchemical mystery was about finding the inner gold of man's soul. Although gold can represent greed and corruption, here at Freaky Dreams Central we prefer to take the view that if you see ingots or bullion or doubloons in your dream, then you, too, are being shown that beautiful inner wealth that's all yours.

GUITAR

(*See* **Musical Instruments**)

THE BEAUTY QUEEN

Madame C.J. Walker (1867—1919), had a dream that resulted in a spectacular double whammy. She became the first female American multi-millionaire, and what is even more glorious and extraordinary, is that she was the first member of her family, all African slaves, to have been born a free woman. In the 1890s Walker was suffering from a common scalp infection which was causing her hair to fall out. She tried all the patented remedies available on the market to no avail. And then she had a dream:

One night I had a dream, and in that dream a big, black man appeared to me and told me what to mix up in my hair. Some of the remedy was grown in Africa, but I sent for it, mixed it, put it on my scalp, and in a few weeks my hair was coming in faster than it had ever fallen out. I tried it on my friends; it helped them. I made up my mind to begin to sell it.

And the solution worked. It's remarkable that all the ingredients were dictated to Madame Walker in this incredible dream. Subsequently, she was able to build her own factory to make the formula and became famed for her work as an entrepreneur and social activist. She was also a much-loved philanthropist, able to do good because the dream recipe made her head of a multi-million dollar empire.

HAIR

Hair is a very important symbolic indicator. Having your hair cut? Then you're saying goodbye to the past. If your hair is long and luscious in your dream, then you're feeling sexually charged. If your hair is unkempt and tangled, however, the opposite is true and you feel your life is a mess. If someone is combing your hair, then you're craving attention in your waking life. A dream of your hair falling out may be accompanied by the same sort of panic as a dream of losing your teeth (*See* page 80). It signifies a perceived loss of strength, control, and virility. However, if you dream that you have white hair, then you are finding inner wisdom.

HAIRBRUSH (*See* **Broom**)

HALL

Remember that houses and rooms represent, generally speaking, aspects of you. What sort of hall is it? Somber and business-like? Or is it full of people having a party? Whatever feeling your dream hall inspires is a reflection of you, so look closely.

HALLOWEEN

Halloween is a feast of the dead, set at the time of year when the "veil" between this world and the next is said to be at its thinnest. Some people believe that spirits communicate in dreams, too, and so there's a possibility that Halloween dreams might contain messages from your own dear departed who are using the familiarity of the festival to get information across to you. If you're not the sort of person that believes in such things, then the trappings of your Halloween dream (grinning pumpkins, apple bobbing, silhouetted witches on broomsticks) are a nostalgic reminder of the carefree days of your childhood, when anything seemed possible.

HALO

To dream of a halo means that you're striving for perfection. If you're wearing the halo, however, it indicates that you think you're perfect.

HANDCUFFS

Restriction, restraining, imprisonment; handcuffs not only mean that your movements are restricted but that your communication options are limited, too; it's hard to write and impossible to gesticulate. But to be handcuffed is also, in a way, to be absolved of authority. When we can't intervene in a situation, we say that "our hands are tied." Although to be handcuffed in your dream might be frustrating, there may also be a rather pleasurable element to it as well. Examine your waking life to find this frustration, and try to determine an upside.

HANDS

Another important bodily symbol, hands are great tools of communication, and of course dreams communicate with us in many diverse ways. Wringing your hands is a sign of anxiety. Hands covered in blood indicate guilt. If the hands are beckoning, then you're being persuaded of something in real life. Waving hands denotes a greeting of hello or goodbye to someone in your waking life. Similarly, a handshake can signify an introduction, a parting, or an agreement. Hands are also used for sign language. If the hands in your dream are "signing" at you, then it could be that your subconscious mind is choosing to tell you something in a rather oblique way.

HARE

Full of magic is the hare. Because of her nocturnal habits, she's associated with the moon and mystical feminine powers. So dreaming of a hare could indicate that you need to get in touch with the feminine or mystical side of yourself.

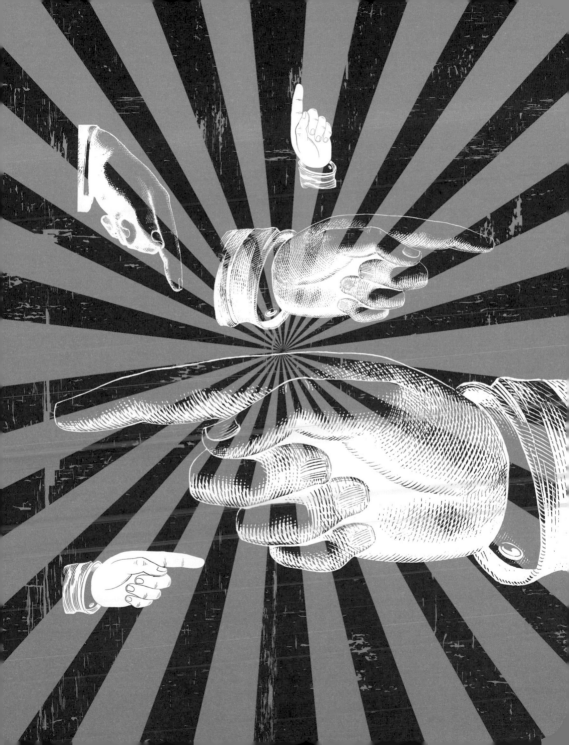

HARVEST

You might dream of the typical food harvest, but the real meaning is that you're harvesting certain things in your life; the culmination of lots of hard work.

HAT

If the cap fits...Hats are a powerful symbol of the role or job of the wearer, and the hats that belong to different professions or vocations are instantly recognizable. Think of a chef's tall white hat, for example; the cap of a sailor or the pointed headgear of a witch. The hat/s in your dream signifies different aspects of yourself but can also act as a disguise; we see the hat and what it signifies rather than the person who's wearing it. If you're wearing a hat that doesn't suit your waking-life profession, you could be considering a new job.

HAWK

Dreaming of a hawk means you need to be on your guard about something in your life. Proceed with caution.

HEAD

This symbolizes the intellect, the conscious mind, authority; to be the "head" is to be the boss. A severed head blasts all these symbolic meanings, and yet the head itself still retains a strong feeling of authority. Just to see a head on its own in a dream would imply that it's floating or possibly even severed in some way. Are you perhaps seeing the severed head of an enemy? Wishful thinking. It's still your enemy, and you need to deal with this relationship properly since the person isn't going to go away. There are several myths from around the world in which an unattached head speaks great wisdom. If this happens in your dream, pay close attention to what it's telling you.

HEADLINE

As with any sort of prominent text appearing in a dream, this is your subconscious mind trying to get a message through to you as clearly as possible. What better way than a newspaper headline? Pay attention, but be aware that the message might be given to you in an oblique manner!

HEART

Context is all when you dream of a heart. Are you seeing a symbolic heart, chocolate-box style? This means you're looking for love in your life. If you're seeing a grizzly heart operation, like a transplant, then there are dramatic changes in matters of your own heart, and you're aware that it might hurt.

HEARING AID

Dreams often compensate for what we're lacking in our everyday life. Therefore, if it's you that's wearing the hearing aid in your dream, then you need to listen more carefully. Someone is trying to tell you something, and you're not paying attention. If it's someone else, then you may feel you're not being heard by this person, and you might want to try a different approach.

HEAVEN

Are you having idealized visions of heaven in your dream? This could indicate that you are dissatisfied with certain aspects of your waking life and you're imagining how they could be in an ideal world. Well, heaven might be lovely but bear in mind it's a one-way location, so to speak. Look to what's good in your life already and you might find that an imaginary vision pales in comparison with the gritty reality of real life.

HEDGE

Vegetable borders appearing prominently in your dream? A hedge can be a boundary marker, or it can be a secure fortification. Only you will know which one applies to your life.

HELL

Some people might say that a dream vision of hell means that you are being taunted by demons. However, it could also be that your dream might represent an aspect of your waking life, something that seems hellish to you, and that you have no control over (job or living situation, perhaps?). However, nothing is generally as bad as we think it is!

HERBS

Can you remember the herb/s that you dreamed about? Herbs are powerful both in magic and medicine, and it might well be that the dreamed of the herbs you need. Otherwise, to dream of herbs is to be made aware of your own capacity to heal, either using herbs directly as medicine or as food.

HERON

If you dream of two herons flying together, this means that your relationship is harmonious and happy. To dream of a lone heron, however, is to face the side of you that is happy with a "hermit" existence.

HIDE-AND-SEEK

If it's you that's doing the hiding and you're playing indoors, take notice of the rooms that you're hiding in; if you're tucked in a tight space, then this indicates you feel you have severe restrictions in your life. If you're hiding in the top of a house, like in the attic, then you could be hiding your emotions behind your intellect. If you're hiding in the basement, then this means you don't want to face up to past events. If you're hiding in the kitchen, then you're afraid of certain social situations. If the game of hide-and-seek is taking place outdoors, you might find refuge in a crumbling old building or shed; this dream is about your need to face up to events in the past that might be coming to the fore. If you're hiding in luxuriant vegetation, you're coming to terms with the earthier side of yourself. If you are the seeker, then in your waking life you're looking for something that's elusive; this elusive item could be something small, such as a lost object, or something bigger, like a partner.

HILL

A hill, or a mountain, signifies achievement and success. If you are climbing the hill, then you're on your way to such wonders. If a hill or a series of hills keeps appearing in your dreams, then it's showing you the obstacles ahead of you in your waking life.

HITLER

An icon of our times, the distinctive figure of the Führer stands for everything that's evil. It stands for fear, hate, and the horror of a totalitarian regime led by one single charismatic and powerful individual who somehow had the wherewithal to convince millions of people to carry out his insane visions. It's also scary to think that this capacity for evil is available to all of us. Strong icons in dreams often represent a side of us. If in your dream you are Hitler, then you're frightened of your capabilities in real life. If you are fighting Hitler, than you are struggling with your own power. Remember that, like electricity, power can be wielded for a number of purposes, not all of them bad.

HOLY GRAIL

The Holy Grail symbolizes an idea, something perfect and quest-worthy. This could indicate that you're on a quest for something equally elusive in your own life. Before you begin your journey, though, make sure it's not right under your nose.

HOMOSEXUALITY

Are you straight, and dreaming that you're homosexual? If the experience leaves you feeling weird, disoriented, and anxious in the morning, then it might be that you need to experiment a little more in your life—not necessarily in a sexual way. Dreams about homosexuality could indicate that your real-life attitude has become a little stale and mundane, and the dream is your subconscious mind trying to remind you that there's a whole big world out there.

HORSE

A typical dream dictionary will tell you that a horse symbolizes power and energy, and this is absolutely true. After all, we still measure the performance of an engine in terms of "horsepower." But did you also know that the horse is a powerful symbol of sex and death, particularly if we're dealing with a stallion (which is effectively the most extreme example of a horse; like a "horse plus"). It's hopefully obvious to you why a stallion should be an erotic symbol, but why should a horse also stand for death?

The thing is, many of our most important symbols ARE so vital because they've been lodged away as such for thousands of years, before we had invented the written word. Many of these ancient images might seem irrational at first glance, but if we dig a little deeper, the reason for the meaning becomes obvious. The horse has been a crucial animal to humankind for thousands of years. Its domestication for man's use meant that we could cover ground very fast, carry goods easily, and also, of course, become more efficient farmers. Effectively, our equine friend was useful to both the hunter and the gatherer.

How about the death thing, though? Again, we've got to look to our collective ancestral memory to find the reason. If you've ever had a horse or been horse riding for any length of time, you'll know all about the close relationship of trust that builds up between human and animal. The horse acts as both friend and ally. So it makes sense to suppose that such a trusted companion would be with us on that final journey into the unknown. In every single society around the world, the horse is what's known as a "psycho pomp"—that is, the horse guides us at the time of death into the next world. And our subconscious minds have way more than a residue of this original emotional attachment.

It's worth mentioning, too, that death, in a dream, never means a plain and simple ending. It means a change. The speed and power of the horse would imply that the change could be both dramatic and powerful.

HORSESHOE

A symbol of luck and also of marriage—seeing the horseshoe in your dream could mean that you'd like to have one or both of these things in your life soon!

HOUSE

An important dream symbol, the house represents aspects of your own psyche as well as the state of mind and your attitudes to certain ideas and concepts. You are the house, effectively. Knowing this, and applying as much objectivity as you possibly can to your dream, makes a house dream relatively easy to analyze. Are there lots of hidden room and secret passages? This would imply that there are aspects of your character that are equally hidden, such as undiscovered talents. Is everything in the house in perfect condition? This indicates that you're very efficient and frequently take care of details, large or small. However, if the house is messy and disheveled, then you need to get yourself in shape, and it's likely that this will be physical as well as mental. If the house is haunted in your dream, then there are certain issues you need to confront and let go of; a personal exorcism.

HURRY

Generally a sign of anxiety, if you are hurrying in your dream, then this means you sometimes worry about things unnecessarily.

HUSBAND

A prominent male character appearing in a dream represents the male side of yourself; the husband in particular is "married" to you, you have chosen one another, and the relationship is freer than that of a blood relative. The husband in the dream represents the male side of you that's a result of your own life choices and decisions.

This dream spouse is a reminder of these choices, and an opportunity to examine them. If you dream of your actual husband, this could be a strong affirmation of the description above. If you see your actual husband engaged in an activity that you wouldn't expect, then you should similarly expect some kind of surprise in your waking life.

HYPNOTIZE

Sometimes dreams allow us to experience behaviors that don't reflect our normal lives. They act as subconscious suggestions or mental breaks. For example, if you're happy to be hypnotized in your dream, this generally indicates that you are a control freak in your waking life. If you're the hypnotist, you need to be more of a control freak in your daily waking life.

"I dreamed of a children's story that features an amazing creature that's half-butterfly and half-mermaid. She's called Buttmaid. Why do I never have dreams that are going to be obvious best sellers?"

ICE

When we "put something on ice," we set it aside—an idea, or whatever it might be—until a later date. To be frozen is to be in an arrested state of development, preserved fresh until the time is right. Dreaming of ice could indicate that there is something in your life that needs to go on the back burner until a later date. The context of your dream should help you figure out what.

ICEBERG

The Titanic sank as a result of two things: an arrogance on behalf of her builders that she was indestructible; and, because of this large chunk of frozen water. There's far more to an iceberg than meets the eye; most of it is hidden beneath the water. Therefore, the iceberg in your dream is very likely to be warning you about something or someone like this. It could be there is someone in your life who isn't showing you their true colors.

IGLOO

If you dream of an igloo and you are an Eskimo in the dream, then this means you are adapting happily to new circumstances in your waking life. If you're not an Eskimo in your dream, but still find yourself surrounded by igloos, then this indicates that you are probably finding your waking environment somewhat strange and uncomfortable. The chill is likely to be down to human factors, though.

ILLNESS

It's always worth taking notice of any sort of dream illness, whether or not the malady is yours. Pay attention to what kind of sickness it is, if you can; sometimes we know there's something wrong, but we mask it beneath a cloak of brusque practicality. This is a warning dream. Go for a check up.

IMPOTENCE

Do you dream that you're sexually impotent? Let's face it, this is more likely to happen if you're a man than a woman, and it's generally something to dread; the whole essence of your masculinity removed at one fell stroke, as it were. But impotence doesn't necessarily only apply to your sexual life, although it's the most glaring

A DREAM INTERRUPTED

It is perhaps ironic that "Kubla Khan" is arguably Samuel Taylor Coleridge's most famous poem, and yet his poem was never completed, and runs to just 54 lines. Coleridge "saw" the poem, complete and intact, in a dream, and had just started to copy it out when he was interrupted by the infamous "person from Porlock" who arrived at the poet's house at Nether Stowey, and stayed for an hour or so. During this visit the great extent of the poem drifted from Coleridge's grasp. Here's how Coleridge described the incident when the poem was first published:

On awakening, he appeared to himself to have a distinct recollection of the whole, and taking his pen, ink, and paper, instantly and eagerly wrote down the lines that are here preserved. At this moment he was unfortunately called out by a person on business from Porlock, and detained by him above an hour, and on his return to his room, found, to his no small surprise and mortification, that though he still retained some vague and dim recollection of the general purport of the vision, yet, with the exception of some eight or ten scattered lines and images, all the rest had passed away like the images on the surface of a stream into which a stone has been cast, but, alas! Without the after, restoration of the latter!

Coleridge was a well-known opium user, and it's been suggested that the poem was inspired by the drug, and that the "person from Porlock" was the poet's dealer.

example of it. The inability to perform in your dream might be an analogy for another part of your life that you feel is impotent: your creativity, your ability to be happy, the failures you see in your job, or the paucity of your bank balance. Have a look at what your dream really means, stop worrying, and start doing something about it. A part of your life needs a shot of metaphorical Viagra.

IMPRISONMENT

If you are imprisoned in a cell of some kind in your dream, then you're feeling trapped in your waking life, and that entrapment is out of your control. That's the *real* prison. If you want to escape your imprisonment, then try lucid dreaming (*see* page 156), and dream up a fabulous escape in which you simply fly from the prison yard, dodging the hail of bullets. It's possible!

INCEST

Unless you're a member of an ancient civilization such as Egypt or Greece, incest is all wrong. Modern moral values place a big fat line through the very thought of having sexual relations with a relative. And yet to dream of incest may give you a hideous thrill despite the taboo status that's attached to even speaking of such a dream. It's likely that there's a side of you that would like to be less conventional, more daring, less worried about what others might think, but that you're afraid to show this part of yourself. Are you repressed? Be more daring, but it doesn't have to go as far as the dream.

INITIALS

If you ever see letters or initials in a dream, then you should try to take note of what they are. Our subconscious mind can give us messages in a slightly skewed way, so the initials might stand for something else; for example B.T. might refer to a person named Betty, or U.C. could be "You See." You see?

INJECTION

Although in your dream you're likely to be being injected with a needle, an "injection" can refer to things other than drugs. We can be given an injection of enthusiasm, for example. Some cars have turbo injection to make them extra powerful. If you're happy with your dream injection, then life is finding a way to give you exactly what you need. If you're unhappy or struggling against the needle, then you are also resisting something that will ultimately be good for you. Have a close look at your life and try to ascertain what this is, and why you're trying to fight it. Immunization is, of course, carried out via the process of injection, too, so there might someone or something that you're looking to protect yourself against.

INK

Ink means permanence. If you're signing your name in ink, it means that you're committing yourself to something—or at least, the dream is allowing you to see what this commitment feels like. If the ink in your dream has spilled, see if it makes a recognizable shape or pattern. There could be a message there. Ink also harks back to an old-fashioned, elegant time, before computers and printers and e-mails. This could mean that a part of you longs for simplicity or a return to tradition.

INSCRIPTION

Any sort of lettering or written message in a dream is usually an example of your subconscious mind trying to tell you something as clearly as possible. However, sometimes the medium can be more powerful than the message, so to speak, and you should also take notice of what the inscription is written on. If it's a cake, for example, you might be expecting a celebration sometime soon. If the engraving is on stone, there are certain truths that you need to acknowledge. If you can't read the inscription clearly, ask your subconscious mind to give you the message again in a clearer way.

INSECTS

Different types of insects signify different things. Ants, for example, denote hard work and team efforts, and this reflects the situation in your own working life. Bees, too, mean that your life is happy and harmonious; seeing bees in your dream could also mean that you're in for a run of good luck. Cockroaches are associated with grubby interiors, which could reflect your anxiety about your messy home,

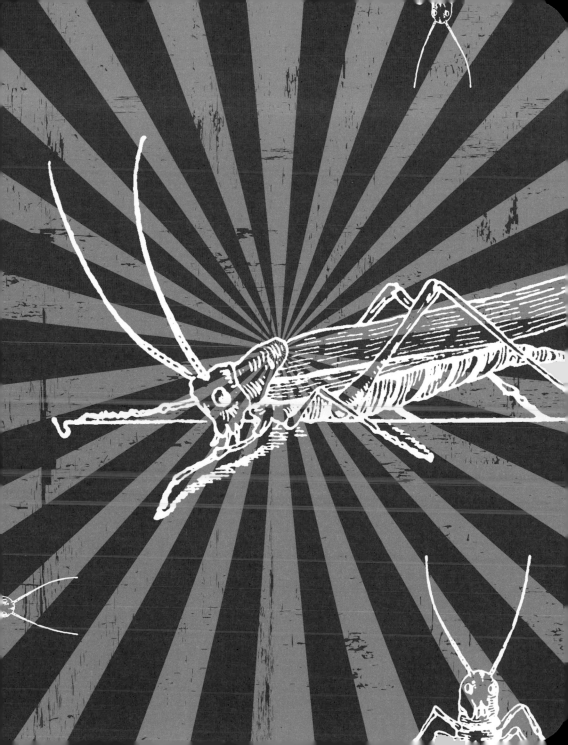

but bear in mind, too, that they will be one of the few creatures that will survive the apocalypse, their shiny outer carapaces protecting them from all sorts of toxic ray guns. The cockroaches of the future will be as big as houses and nasty as heck. If you're dreaming of these gigantic cockroaches, then perhaps the planet is doomed. Or maybe they're indeterminate insects, crawling all over you and making you itch? Perhaps you're sleeping in sheets containing too many man-made fibers. Flies are symbolic of death and destruction, and seeing lots of them is a typical anxiety dream, meaning that you need to address your worries head-on in your waking life. (*See* also the entries for **Spider** and **Web**.)

INSIDE-OUT CLOTHES

Did you know that wearing your clothes inside out was once considered to be a very effective way of confounding the fairies and throwing them off track? Wearing your clothing inside out is a real finger up to authority, and if this is what you're doing in your dream, then this could

be your subconscious advising you to carry a little more of this feisty attitude forward in your waking life.

IRON

Iron is one of the sacred metals, and we used to believe that it acted as a sort of kryptonite to fairies and other supernatural creatures, keeping them away. Therefore, there's a protective aspect to iron. Seeing it in your dream means that you are "protected" in your waking life. If the iron is rusty and rotting, though, there's something in your life that isn't as powerful as it used to be. This could apply to a person, a situation, or even yourself.

INTERCOM

Spiritualists believe that if you're receiving messages from an intercom, then they're coming from a deceased loved one, from the other side of the veil. Whether or not this is the case, the intercom is also an effective way for your subconscious mind to make contact with you. The message you receive may not be direct, though, so some unscrambling might be in order.

INTRUDER

Is there someone in your house that shouldn't be there? If the intruder is scary, this could be an indication that there is someone in your life, possibly at work, that is threatening your domain. If you feel like you should welcome the intruder in your dream, an intruder can also signify aspects of ourselves that we maybe didn't know about. These could be hidden talents!

INVISIBILITY

To dream that you are invisible might mean that you're feeling neglected, unnoticed, and taken for granted in your everyday life.

ISLAND

An island signifies isolation. This is an indication that your life might benefit from a little alone time. Look at it as a way of replenishing your batteries and getting some headspace. It doesn't have to be an actual island so much as a state of mind.

IVY

Ivy signifies the feminine element and is also evergreen. To dream of ivy means that there is likely an evergreen lady in your life who tends to be clingy.

JACKET (*See* **Clothing**)

JACK-IN-THE-BOX

If you have fond memories of a jack-in-the-box as a child, then this could be a nostalgic dream indicating a desire to return to innocent and easier times. But these toys can be pretty scary and creepy. If you were frightened by the jack-in-the-box in your dream, then it's also possible that you're in for a surprise in your waking life.

JAIL (*See* **Prison**)

JEALOUSY

Are you feeling jealous of anything in particular in your dream, or is it less specific than that? Jealous is a byproduct of insecurity, and however much you might protest your own emotional stability, jealous feelings in a dream tell a very different story. You should examine your feelings closely in your waking life and avoid suppressing your emotions.

JEANS (*See* **Clothing**)

JEDI

Recently, when the census returns came in for the population of England and Wales, 0.8% of people stated their religion as "Jedi," surpassing Buddhism, Jainism, and Sikhism. Quite a result for the quasi-religious knights of the fictional *Star Wars* sagas. We all know what the Jedi stands for: truth, honesty, and a great reliance on mystical and instinctual powers. It's not surprising that more and more people find such honorable values appearing in their dreams, in the guise of the Jedi. If the Jedi appears in your dream, he's there as a reminder that there are answers to your problems in both ancient wisdom and in modern philosophical literature.

JELL-O

While it's more commonly associated with its partner in crime, peanut butter, Jell-O is also a euphemism for a person who has no "oomph," no backbone; someone who is easily persuaded. Seeing Jell-O in a dream could mean this euphemism applies to you, or to someone you know. Harmless and sweet, but kind of useless.

JESUS

It's almost impossible to remove Jesus as a personality from Christ as a religious figure. There have been millions of words of analysis into his character as a human being, but it's fair to say he was a highly controversial political figure as well as being a healer and philosopher. In what context does he appear in your dream? Whether or not you're not a staunch Christian, the likelihood, nevertheless, is that you will regard the appearance of such a powerful and auspicious figure as something to be taken seriously. It is a good omen to see Jesus in a dream as it indicates that you will get through troubled times with strength and forbearance. Bear in mind those legendary healing powers too; Jesus' appearance in a dream could mean that you, too, have talents in this area.

JET

If you're dreaming of a jet plane, it could be that you're feeling highly energized or that events in your life are moving at a colossally fast pace. It could also indicate that there is a trip in your future; leaving on a jet plane? Alternately, Whitby Jet is a black-hued mineral that, when highly polished and faceted, was much in demand by the Victorians, who had an epidemic fascination for all things to do with death and mourning. Perhaps you're mourning something in your life, too, if this is the jet that appears in your dream.

JEWELS

This is generally a good dream. All the different valuable gems and jewels that you see are actually aspects of *you*, wonderful you! Acknowledge the fact that you are beautiful, talented, valuable; positively jewel like.

It's unlikely that the jewels are being taken away from you, but if they are, then the dream is telling you that you should be on your guard against people that might be taking advantage of your good nature. Perhaps you're being underpaid for your talents and efforts? Only one person can fix this injustice.

JIGSAW PUZZLES

The incoherent pieces of a jigsaw puzzle combine together to make a coherent whole. With a real-life jigsaw puzzle, we can refer back to the box lid to see what's going on in the picture. If you dream of a jigsaw puzzle, however, you're dreaming of all the incoherent pieces of your own life and trying to make sense of them. In many ways, you might think it's a shame that you don't have a picture to refer to. But then if you knew exactly what was going on in the jigsaw puzzle that is your own life, how tedious would that be?

JOB

Even if your job is highly charged and highly paid, you wouldn't necessarily want to spend 24 hours per day thinking about it. If your work life impinges on your sleeping life, then it's possible that you could be optimizing your waking, working hours more effectively. It's also likely that you could be spending too much of your waking life on your job; leaven the load with more of a social life, including sports activities.

JOCKEY

To dream you're riding a horse is to know that you are in charge of your own destiny. To dream that you are a racing jockey is even more so; the speed and danger involved, and the elevated position on the back of a very fast horse, shows that you're seriously in control of matters in your life.

JOKER

It is interesting to dream of playing cards of any type, since each individual card carries a great deal of significance. The Joker translates into the Fool of the tarot, and stands for endless possibilities; a childlike state where we simply have no limits. Seeing this card in your dream is a reminder that this state of mind is accessible to you as well as the possibilities. If someone you know appears as the Joker in your dream, then you could be seeing the true nature of this person, since the Joker is also a master of disguise. Proceed with caution.

JOURNAL

If you dream of a journal, be alert; this could be a very informative dream. It is entirely possible that you find yourself on the brink of a prophecy dream, in which you're writing about future events in the journal. Or you might be writing about past events in such a way that you have a greater understanding of them. Remember that dreams are sometimes skewed, and so the contents of the journal—should you be lucky enough to be able to read it— might be slightly scrambled.

JOURNEY

Life itself is a journey—isn't it? So to dream that you're on a journey means that you are appraising your life as a whole. Forward motion and expansion are inevitable, but the journey dream also allows you to take stock of where you are along the road. For you to properly understand this dream will require a degree of detachment, an ability to see your own life as from above.

JUDGE

If you're seeing a typical courtroom judge in your dream, then it's possible that you yourself might be feeling judged—particularly if you're standing in the courtroom dock. It's also possible that you might need to apply better judgment to a particular situation in your own life. But remember to be kind to yourself in the process; we often tend to judge ourselves far more harshly than we judge others.

FAMOUS FREAKY DREAMERS
PROPHECIES OF DOOM

If you had a dream that implied you'd be pushing up the daisies sometime soon, that probably wouldn't be very comforting. Chances are, though, that you wouldn't record it in any way. You might mention it to a friend to dispel the trauma, and then after that, you'd probably forget all about it. And yet there have been occasions when such dreams have actually come true. Not very many of these dreams survive, admittedly, because the odds stacked against proving it are very high indeed. Think about it.

You need to have the dream—and remember it—in the first place. You would need to record it in such a way that makes it accessible after your demise, so you'd probably need a witness. The dream would actually need to come true. After all these points have been met, you'd probably still need to have some kind of public persona otherwise no-one would give a damn. This might seem harsh, but we live in a celebrity culture.

CALIGULA

In view of the points above, consider poor Caligula. Hardly one of nature's Mr. Nice Guys, this vicious Roman emperor must have been pretty mad when he dreamed one night that he was standing before the throne of Jupiter (implying power and riches) only to be kicked back down the stairs, so to speak, by God. We can only wonder if this depressing dream haunted him all day and was the last thing that occurred to him as he was assassinated later that night.

ABRAHAM LINCOLN

Former U.S. President, Abraham Lincoln, like Caligula, was assassinated. And a dream predicted that assassination. Evidently, Abe Lincoln held great store by the messages in his dreams, and described how certain dreams presaged "big" events. But none as big as the dream he described to his wife.

Here's what he told her:

..There seemed to be death-like stillness about me. Then I heard subdued sobs, as if a number of people were weeping. I thought I left my bed and wandered downstairs. There the silence was broken by the same pitiful sobbing, but the mourners were invisible. I went from room to room; no living person was in sight, but the same mournful sounds of distress met me as I passed along. It was light in all the rooms; every object was familiar to me; but where were all the people who were grieving as if their hearts would break? I was puzzled and alarmed. What could be the meaning of all this? Determined to find the cause of a state of things so mysterious and so shocking, I kept on until I arrived at the East Room, which I entered. There I met with a sickening surprise. Before me was a catafalque, on which rested a corpse wrapped in funeral vestments. Around it were stationed soldiers who were acting as guards; and there was a throng of people, some gazing mournfully upon the corpse, whose face was covered, others weeping pitifully. "Who is dead in the White House?" I demanded of one of the soldiers "The President" was his answer; "he was killed by an assassin!" Then came a loud burst of grief from the crowd, which awoke me from my dream...

One wonders if there was anything that Lincoln could have done to avert disaster, whether the dream could have been treated as a warning, not a prophecy. One person who did treat such a dream as a warning is Adolf Hitler.

HITLER

When Hitler was an infantryman during the First World War, he was asleep in a trench when he was awakened by a dream. In the dream, he saw the trench filled with molten metal and blood-splattered earth. Taking this as a warning, he took himself elsewhere. Shortly after he did so, the trench was indeed hit by a mortar and the vision of twisted metal and gore became a reality. It's a hideous irony that, because he paid attention to a dream, Hitler would become the future Fuhrer, responsible for the murder of millions of people and the ghastliest war ever endured on this Earth.

"I'm looking for the fairies. I HAVE to find the fairies. They're not fairies as in fairies with wings, but fairies as in proper magic little people, the old type. I can hear their voices but I can't see them."

JUGGLING

Besides the circus performance act, when we speak of "juggling" things we mean, metaphorically speaking, that we are trying to keep many diverse things in the air at any one time. The implication being, of course, that if any one item hits the deck, then it's smashed to bits—a disaster. If you dream of juggling, it might be better to selectively put down a few of the items that you are trying to balance, in order to avert such a calamity. If you're juggling balls, however, it could be time to let go and see just how high they can bounce!

JUNGLE

Are you lost in a dream jungle, unsure of which way to turn, afraid that there could be dangerous animals lurking behind the trees? The jungle itself represents those parts of your life that are uncivilized, untamed, and unknown. The "jungle" also represents similar aspects of your character. It's good to dream that you're in the jungle, because it means that now is the time for you to take a walk on the wild side.

JUNK

Rubbish, trash, garbage, refuse, junk... whatever you call it, in a dream this represents exactly what it does in our everyday life; the stuff that we no longer need and that needs to be discarded. Not just physical objects but ideas, relationships, and connections to the past that we might have trouble letting go.

JURY (See also **Judge**)

If you dream of a jury, there are two scenarios. If you are a member of the jury, then this means you are passing judgment on to others in your waking life. If you are standing before a jury, however, then someone is passing judgment on you. So the first thing you need to determine is how the jury appears in the dream—and remember, dreams are neither logical nor are they obvious. You also need to ask yourself why would you be judged and what for; or, alternatively, why do you find yourself in a situation of passing judgment? Think critically about recent events in your life.

KABBALAH

The mysteries of the Kabbalah operate on a different level from the normal everyday reality that we take for granted. It's multileveled and multilayered, ancient, impeccably fascinating, and the structures inherent within it lend themselves to the dream world. If you're very lucky, you may find that your dream gives you a wordless, instinctive understanding of the arcane occult beauty of the Kabbalah. Otherwise, this dream is telling you that there are mysteries in your own life that you might want to explore.

KARAOKE

For some people, the thought of taking part in a karaoke session is as horrifying as taking your clothes off in public. Others, meanwhile, can't wait to grab hold of the microphone. In your waking life you could be either, but whichever you are will have no bearing on your dream. To dream that you're taking part in karaoke is a reminder that you need to take to the stage, metaphorically speaking, in your waking life. You've been part of the audience for too long, so have courage!

KENNEL

A kennel is obviously a doghouse. So if you're the one in a kennel, then you feel that you're in disgrace for some reason. It could also indicate that perhaps you're feeling a little overcrowded in your own house.

KETTLE (See Teapot)

KEY

A key can unlock all sorts of things in addition to locks. We talk of the key to a heart, for example. A key is also a sort of an answer, an essential tool for getting to the next part of an equation. Keys also represent responsibility (house key, car key, office key, etc.). The bigger the bunch of keys, the more burdensome they are, implying authority, ownership of property, and all the advantages and disadvantages that these materialistic trappings bring. So if you dream about a big bunch of keys, it could mean that you have responsibilities that are making you nervous in your waking life. If you dream that you've lost your keys, then this indicates a similar feeling of a loss

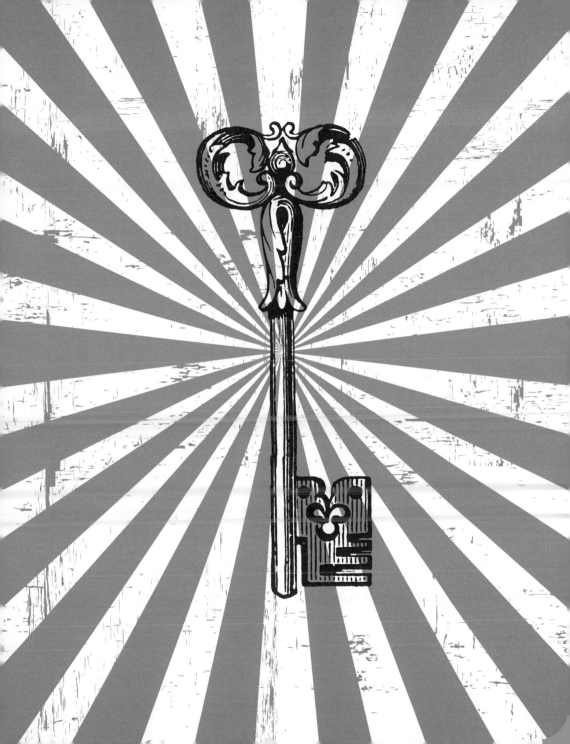

of status in your real life. The key also has obvious sexual connotations, so examine the context of the key or keys in your dream to see which one applies.

KEYHOLE

Though it seems like a simple place, a keyhole is a magical, luminal area, a place between two worlds, a little no-mans' land through which we can access secrets. If you're looking through a keyhole in your dream, you could have stumbled upon a secret in your waking life, or you could be curious about what's coming next in your life and trying to find ways to deduce what these things might be.

KICKING

If you're being kicked in your dream— particularly if you're being kicked in the head—it's possible that your subconscious mind is trying to tell you something important. If you're being kicked in the chest (near the heart), then you need to get in touch with your emotions. If you are kicking someone else, then you're trying to find a way to grab that person's attention in real life.

KIDNAP

Are you kidnapping someone in your dream? This could indicate that your methods of persuasion are not very good in your waking life. It could also denote your frustration at not being able to express yourself properly. If you're the one being kidnapped, however, then it's possible that you feel oppressed, frustrated, and helpless by certain events in your life at this time.

KILL (*See* **Murder**)

KILT

Clothes, in dreams, show our status, or at least the way in which we would like to appear to others. If you're a man and you're wearing a kilt in a dream, then you feel a strong allegiance to the "tribe" of men that are a part of your life.

KING

If you dream of a king that isn't you, then this king could represent your boss, your father, or a similar patriarchal figure for whom you have respect. After all, a king is a figure of supreme authority. If you are being crowned as a king—whatever your sex—you might feel daunted by certain responsibilities in your waking life. Alternately, you might feel that your time in the sun has arrived. Your emotional reaction to the dream will help you determine which one applies to you.

KISSING

If you're about to kiss someone in a dream, but wake up before the moment of connection, then you're not alone. This is a very popular dream, and it indicates frustration at not being able to attain what you desire in real life. It's not unlikely that you're yearning for some physical action, but there is something stopping you from achieving it. Don't be shy! If, however, you dream that you are actually kissing someone that you really like, this is your dream effectively fulfilling a wish for you. If you find that you're kissing something or someone whom you find repugnant, how do you feel? Disgust might be your natural reaction that would mirror your real feelings, but if you find you're enjoying yourself, then an unexpected event will soon happen in your life.

KITE

If you're flying a kite in clear, breezy conditions in your dreams, then this is good. It shows that your ideas, like the kite, are "taking off," and yet you remain grounded and focused. If the sky is gray or cloudy, and the kite is racing turbulently up above you,

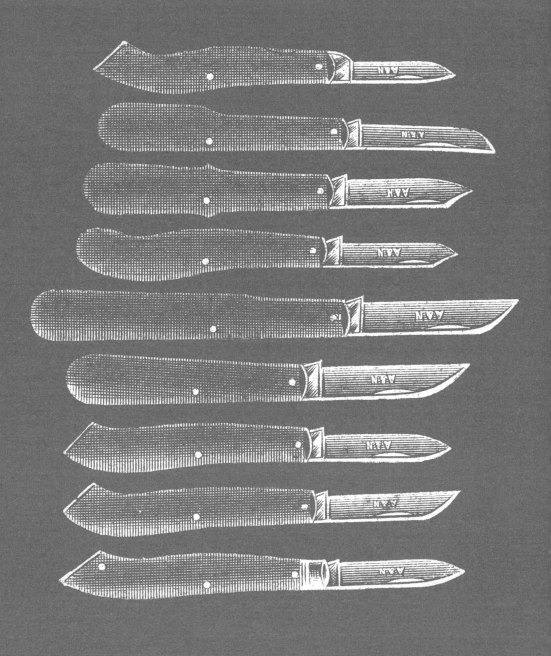

then you might be overwhelmed with responsibilities that you're still trying to hang onto. If you're struggling to get the kite off the ground, then this applies to a situation in your real life— be it a relationship or your career. If you're a man, this could also be a sign of sexual difficulties.

KNEELING

A gesture of submission and humility. If it's you that is kneeling in the dream, this could be an indication that you're in a position of submission in your life. If someone is kneeling before you, well done. Use your power wisely and kindly.

KNIFE

A knife might be a weapon, but it's also a symbol. Like the sword, it symbolizes the clean, swift sharpness of an ending and of a new beginning. If the blade of the knife is rusted or corroded, however, that ending might be a bit messy. If you are handling a knife in the dream, then you need to be aware of both the state of the knife and the context. If you are trying to hurt someone with the knife, it could

be that you are angry and frustrated with a person or a situation in your waking life.

KNIGHT

Is this a white knight that appears in your dreams, ready to sweep you away in his arms? Dream on, since this will never happen in real life. For starters, most knights have their faces covered so you won't be able to check the goods. Secondly, this is wishful thinking in the extreme, a dream of escapism and reflects a desire for you to be "rescued." If it's a black knight in your dream, then you have an unknown enemy.

KNOTS

Generally speaking, knots symbolize problems, mix-ups, and entanglements in your life. But your dream may be of the beautifully constructed sailors' knots that are not only useful, but also works of art. If so, then you might be craving similar artistic and practical perfection in your own life.

FAMOUS FREAKY DREAMERS
KEKULE,
THE SLEEPING SCIENTIST

Sometimes we're fortunate enough to have a dream happen exactly when we need it to. But Frederick August Kekule von Stradonitz, a Belgian scientist, was lucky enough to have this happen twice during his lifetime. Both times his fortuitous dreams resulted in vital discoveries in the world of organic chemistry. Kekule's fame was so extraordinary that he even appeared on the stamps in his home country.

One of the visions evidently came to him while he was on a bus journey, since he tells us that the dream was interrupted by the conductor announcing "Clapham Road." After nodding off, Kekule saw atoms dancing before his eyes, revealing their structure to him very clearly. This resulted in the formulation of his theory of chemical structure.

Later, when Kekule was struggling with his notebooks, he again dozed off in front of his fire. This time, the dancing atoms showed him the information he needed to complete his research into the structure of benzene. Here's how he described the process:

...I was sitting writing on my textbook, but the work did not progress; my thoughts were elsewhere. I turned my chair to the fire and dozed. Again the atoms were gamboling before my eyes. This time the smaller groups kept modestly in the background. My mental eye, rendered more acute by the repeated visions of the kind, could now distinguish larger structures of manifold conformation; long rows sometimes more closely fitted together all twining and twisting in snake-like motion. But look! What was that? One of the snakes had seized hold of its own tail, and the form whirled

mockingly before my eyes. As if by a flash of lightning I awoke; and this time also I spent the rest of the night in working out the consequences of the hypothesis.

There are two aspects to Kekule's experience that are particularly noteworthy. One, that after concentrating hard on the matter in question, he allowed his thoughts to wander, and nodded off. This gave his subconscious mind the opportunity it needed to offer up a solution. Secondly, like many dreams, the image of the twisting snake revealed, if obliquely, the very structure he'd been investigating. That's why it's crucial to look for the hidden messages of your dreams.

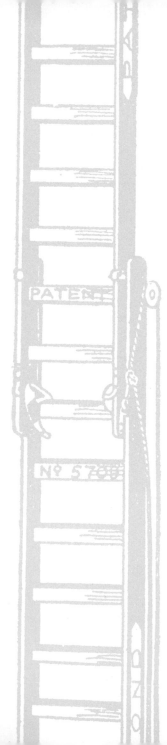

LABYRINTH

The labyrinth or maze in your dream signifies difficult decisions that need to be made. The walls of the maze might suggest that you feel that you don't have enough information to make an informed decision—perhaps this is something that you need to bear in mind.

LADDER

The ladder has its base in the earth and its top, effectively, in the heavens, and so it often symbolizes a spiritual journey; it frequently appears in religious iconography. If you are climbing a ladder, then you're anticipating success and all good things. If you are descending the ladder, then perhaps you realize that you need to literally "take a few steps back" from the situation you're in, and that you need a period of consolidation before you try to hit the heights again. To walk under a ladder traditionally signifies bad luck, but only if you're superstitious. If you dream of walking under a ladder, then you're considering taking a big risk with something in your life.

LADYBUG

It's an interesting phenomenon that sometimes small things are shown to us in dreams in intense magnification. The lovely red body and shiny black dots of the ladybug makes it a favorite with children, and to see this insect in your dreams is a reminder to you to look at the world with the same sense of wonder as a child.

LAKE

Water in general represents the female element—the unknown, the deep. If the lake in your dream is calm and unruffled, then this reflects your inner state. If, however, the water is choppy, cut up by the winds, then your emotional state is similarly ruffled.

LAMP

Any light source in a dream is generally an aspect of the spiritual, rather than material. A brightly lit lamp is either a reminder that your spiritual side is shining bright, or alternatively it could be a reminder to nurture that aspect; you'll know which from the "feeling" of the dream. A lamp that gives off a dim light tells you that your energies have been somewhat depleted.

LANDSLIDE

Landslides are one of the "disaster" dreams, and so it carries much of the same symbolism as avalanches—a cascade of events in your waking life seem to be overwhelming, too much to handle, and uncontrollable. You need to wrest some space and distance for yourself to be able to assess what the damage is—if any!

LANGUAGES

Have you ever had a dream in which someone is trying to tell you something in a foreign language? If this makes you feel anxious and bewildered, the linguistic confusion means that there's something similar happening in your waking life; there's a person, or people, who are not "speaking the same language" as you. If you're trying to tell someone something, and they are having problems understanding you, then maybe you need to think again about how you're trying to explain things. Sometimes pictures can be a better "language" than mere words.

LASSO

If someone is trying to capture you with a lasso or if you are actually lassoed, this dream implies that you feel that your life isn't your own and that you're being forced to do things against your will. You need to wrest back control over your life. If, on the other hand, you're the cowboy with the looped rope, you're trying to keep something close to you that you should probably set free—for both of your sakes.

LATE

Being late is a typical anxiety dream. Only you can know the source of this dream, but it might be a good idea to look closely at the causes of anxiety in your waking life and try to allay them. Things might not be as bad as you think. If you're feeling that there's simply not enough time to do all the things you want to do, then it's time to cut away the dead wood.

LATIN

You might see something in your dream that's written in Latin. Do your best to remember what the letters are. Your subconscious mind could be using this ancient language—which permeates our own tongue despite its "dead" status—to impart a message to you.

LAVA

Hot molten lava is the result of a volcano, the fallout, if you like. If you dream of lava, this is a sign that the worst has happened and things will improve, but in the meantime, tread carefully.

LAWN

If your dream lawn is beautifully manicured, this could be a sign that all is healthy with your life. If it is perfectly manicured and yet feels strange, this could be a sign that things are slightly too perfect. If the grass is dry and parched, then you need to take care of something very close to home—so close that the problem is right under your feet, so to speak.

LEASH

If you are leading someone or something on your dream leash, then you need to feel more in control of things in your waking life, although here at Freak Dreams Central we wouldn't recommend that you demonstrate this by tying a piece of rope around someone's neck. If you're the one on the end of the lead, then you need to consider some of the choices you're currently making in your life. Someone could be leading you astray. If the creature you're taking care of has escaped its leash, this is an anxiety dream. You are afraid of relinquishing control.

LEDGE

If you're standing on the ledge in your dream, then it could be that in your waking life you feel in a precipitate state, like everything around you is suddenly rushing forward without haste. However, in dreams, you can fly. If you're seeing someone you know on a ledge, this might be an anxiety dream but it might also reflect your feelings and intuitions about this person's situation in waking life. Speak to them and ask if you can help.

LEGS

Legs are a symbol of solidity, stability, and strength. If they feature prominently in your dream, then it could be that you need some of this simple stability in your life. If the legs in your dream are broken, then there are recent events in your life that have destabilized and shocked you. It's good to process these things; it shows that you're ready to deal with things and move on.

LESBIAN

Whether you're a man or a woman, gay or straight, to dream of a lesbian—or that you are one—indicates a need to embrace all aspects of yourself and your sexuality and to liberate yourself from inhibitions, mentally at the very least.

LETTER

If you dream about a letter, then interesting and intriguing new developments and news are coming your way. It's also likely that you're ready for a change in your life, and the universe is about to fix this for you. Remember to embrace new opportunities, whatever their nature. If you see an initial, as in the form of a letter of the alphabet, you need to decipher what that initial might mean. A person? A situation? It could be anything, but often the first thought is the best thought.

LEVITATION

Close to flying dream, if you are levitating in your sleeping world, it is a likely precursor to your dream becoming lucid. (*See* page 156 for more on **Lucid Dreaming**.)

LIBRARY

A library is a depository full of books, and books are full of knowledge. Therefore, to dream of library means there is a situation in your life that requires you to better equip yourself with information before you make any move.

LIGHTBULB

A dream lightbulb symbolizes a sudden light , like inspiration. It's no accident that a picture of a lightbulb is often used as the symbol for an idea. Open yourself up to inspiration!

LIGHTHOUSE

As well as being a guide in the darkness, a lighthouse is a classic phallic symbol. Only you will know which is the most relevant. Perhaps both?

LINGERIE (See Bra)

LION

Lions are traditionally a symbol of strength, and despite their ferocity there is something comforting about them. If the lion is attacking you in your dream, then you need to acknowledge your own power. To dream of a lioness, on the other hand, signifies fierce maternal love and protection.

LIPS

Lips are an important opening. They speak; they eat; they kiss. And they spit. What aspect best defines the lips that you're seeing in your dream? Broadly speaking, whatever it is, it's something that's missing from your life. Maybe you need to speak up. Maybe you need to eat. Maybe you need to be kissed. Remember that all these things can be metaphorical as well as physical.

LIZARD

Interesting animals are reptiles. They signify the animal side of our nature, the instinct, the parts that exist outside of the realms of words and the intellect. If you dream of a lizard, then you need to be closer in touch with this primal, instinctive side of yourself.

LOCKET

To dream of a locket is to dream about secrets. Someone you know has a secret—or it could be that you're keeping something a secret. If the locket in your dream is open or being forced open, then the dream is telling you that it's time to open this secret to the world. In general, honesty is the best policy!

LOST

If in your dreamscape you are lost, what's the environment? If it's alienating and strange, then in your waking life you could be feeling that you're entirely in the wrong place at the wrong time. If it feels somehow familiar—that you're lost in a place that you seem to recognize—then it could be time for you to address things from the past that, until now, you've been processing subconsciously.

LOTTERY

To dream of a lottery or lottery ticket—especially if you're given the ticket or if you're drawing the lottery—is to be informed by that good old subconscious mind that it's time for you to take your fate into your own hands. Anything is possible; you are your own winning ticket, so take a chance!

LOVE

How do you dream of an emotion? If you feel emotional in your dream, then you might find that you're on the brink of a "lucid" dream (See page 156). It's a matter of practice for you to be able to make that leap into conscious "dreaming." However, if you have fond dreams of a past love, then it might be that there's unfinished business that your relationship isn't yet over. The form this relationship takes in the future, however, will be different. If you dream that you are in love with a shadowy stranger, then you're longing for love in your waking life. Get

yourself out there and find him or her! If you dream that you're in love with someone "forbidden," like the spouse of a friend, it's likely that your dream is showing you your true feelings—feelings that you wouldn't even admit to in real life.

LUNCH

To dream that you are eating any sort of meal usually indicates that you need nourishment—but not necessarily of the edible variety. Examine the spiritual part of your life since this, too, needs sustenance and "feeding."

LUTE

Any kind of musical instrument appearing in a dream usually symbolizes harmony and spirituality. If you can hear the music, this makes the symbolism ever stronger. The lute speaks of ancient days and ancient wisdom. If the music is disharmonious, then you need to investigate the causes of such emotional and spiritual discord in your waking life. If the music is relaxing and harmonious, then your waking spirituality is strong.

LUCID DREAMING: THE ART OF CONTROLLING YOUR DREAMS

It is a waste of good dreaming time if we don't get to enjoy the odd lucid dream now and then. So what exactly is a lucid dream?

If you've ever had one, you'll know instantly. If not, then you don't know what you're missing! Lucid dreams have a super-real quality, but the main difference between a lucid dream and a "normal" dream is that at some point in the dream we actually realize that we are dreaming, and, so long as we don't pitch ourselves back into the real world at the excitement of it all, we can control those dreams to a certain extent. Flying is a favorite pastime for those lucky enough to have frequent lucid dreams.

To paraphrase Carl Jung, when our subconscious mind knows that we want to play, it will play back with us. Here are some tips which should help you to dream lucidly—but keep trying if it doesn't happen the first time. It's seriously worth it.

1. During the day, take time out to really notice your surroundings. Look around closely; notice anything that might seem unfamiliar about a familiar environment. Make a deliberate effort to take a mental snapshot of a particular aspect of wherever you are; look at things as though you were a tourist in your own life. Do this 4 or 5 times a day.

2. Find a strong scent or any distinctive smelling substance—ground coffee, cinnamon, whatever. Concentrate on a particular object at the same time as inhaling the aroma of whatever it is that you've chosen.

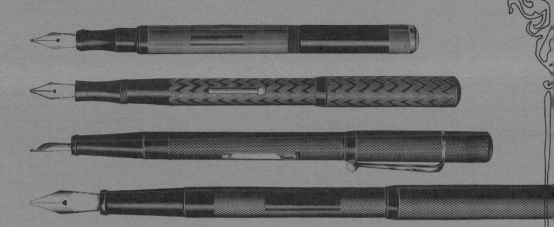

3. The first rule of dream analysis is keeping an open notebook with a (working) pen by your bed. Make sure this is ready before going to sleep.

4. Before drifting off to sleep, recall the snapshots that you took in your mind earlier that day. Then think of the object at the same time as inhaling the aroma.

5. Go to sleep, and see what happens next. You may find that you snap into lucidity immediately; you might not. Keep trying though. This is something you can practice to achieve.

This account is from Alex, born in North Carolina but now living in Scotland.

The only time I ever really remember dreams is when I write them down. A few days ago I came across an old dream diary that I'd kept when I was in my teens. In the notebook, I wrote in great detail, about a rug that was beside my bed. The rug was a photograph of a moving landscape.

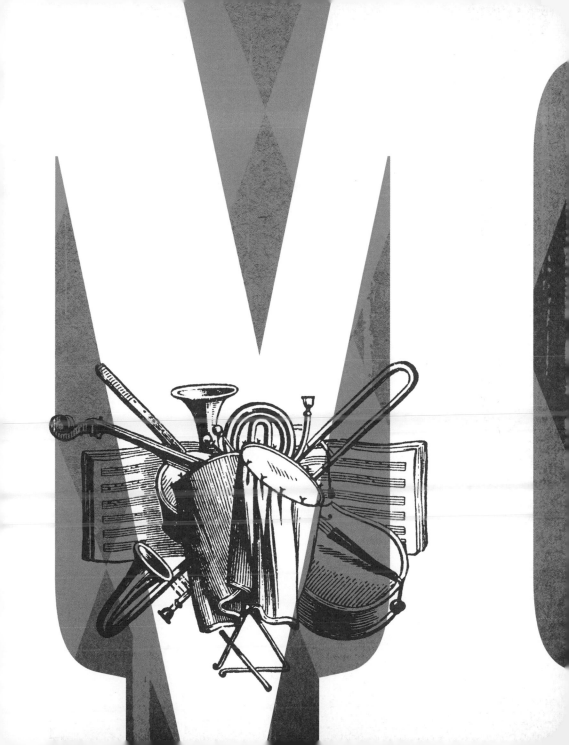

MACHINES

Machines, machinery, mechanical objects—they operate without the need for thought or emotion; without a soul. When we say that someone is a "machine," we mean that they operate strictly according to the rules, always on time, highly efficient, and unchanging despite any fluctuation in the surrounding circumstances. Such a dream might mean that your own life, although highly efficient in many ways or most of the time, might have recently suffered an organizational setback. Can you keep all that disciplined efficiency and still have a little fun?

MADONNA (See Virgin Mary)

MAGGOTS

More the stuff of nightmares than dreams, maggots appear where there is dead flesh to feed on. Is there a metaphorical form of dead flesh in your life? Perhaps it's time to turn those maggots onto the dead or dying aspect in your life and begin anew.

MAGNIFYING GLASS

If you're looking at things up close with a magnifying glass in your dream, this is an indication that there are certain elements of your own life that are also being closely scrutinized.

MAIL

Giving, receiving, or otherwise seeing mail in your dream is all about communication. The appearance of this symbol could mean that your ability to communicate in real life has become difficult or has become restricted in some capacity. Seek out different methods of getting your point across.

MAKEUP

Makeup is all about changing and altering your appearance. Sometimes makeup can act as a sort of mask, disguising what's really underneath. If you see yourself in a mirror with heavy makeup on, for example, then you need to ask yourself whether you are being as open, confident, and forthright as you could be in your waking life. If you

see a friend wearing heavy makeup, then maybe you're aware that the person has something to hide. If you see yourself or another person wearing no makeup, then the dream is showing you vulnerability and honesty. If you see a man wearing makeup, then there are certain things in your waking life that you need to question.

MAKING OUT

Many dreams of sexual liaisons speak of unfulfilled sexual desires in your waking life. Making out is the province of the spotty teenager, and it might be that you're longing for a return to those innocent times of puppy love and new adventures rather than a lasting commitment.

MANDALA

A mandala is effectively a sort of spiritual map, its circular shape and internal patterns and colors a plan of the universe, material and spiritual, internal and external. To see such a mandala in your dream is a call to that spiritual journey, which will both enrich your waking life and nourish the part of you that dreams. It's also worth noting whether there are any particularly prominent colors or shapes in the mandala. If there are, please see the **Color** entry on page 56.

MANSION

Any "container" in a dream is representative of you and your psyche. And though it is an elaborate container, a mansion falls under this category. Since mansions evoke notions of grandness, wealth, power, importance, excess, and the need to be served, then these qualities are all aspects of you. If you are wandering from room to room in your dream, feeling lost and mystified by locked doors and the maze of rooms, then there are aspects of yourself that you have yet to explore and understand. Those locked rooms are the darker parts of your psyche that will unlock when you are ready.

MAP

How exciting! A map charts unknown or unfamiliar territory. You never know what you're going to find there—the beauty is in the not knowing. Then again, to see a map of a place you've never been to in your dream is to see a series of potential clues indicating not only physical territory, but also the territory of the past, the present, and the future. And, of course, maps very often show the way to hidden treasure! The tricky part of a map dream is in being able to deduce what's actually on the map in the first place. If you dream about a map of a place you've already been to, then you've been thinking of the past lately.

MARIJUANA

This herb carries the symbolism of rebellion, anarchy, and anti-authoritarianism as well as the effects of the chemicals contained within it; psychedelic experiences, trippiness, all those things we know about "wacky baccy." Assuming you're a fine upstanding citizen and never touch the stuff, then if you dream of smoking marijuana, this is an indication that you need to loosen up a little, relax, and bend the rules occasionally in some part of your life.

MARKET

Here, many things are laid before you all of them available for the right price—or, indeed, often for less than the right price since haggling is a regular part of market trading. All the things that you encounter in the dream market are things that are available to you. The problem is that when there's so much choice, it can be hard to make a decision. This dream serves to underline that you might be having trouble making a decision. Try to remember if you are drawn to something in your dream market that might help you make your choice.

MARSHMALLOW

Eating marshmallows often allows us to go back to a state of childlike innocence, a time when things were easy and simple. When do we stop toasting marshmallows, and why? It could be that your dream is telling you to embrace such childlike simplicity once again. The soft and spongy texture of the marshmallow, and its sweetness, carries erotic overtones, and your dream reveals a longing for sensual pleasures in your life.

MASK

Masks disguise us. They give us an alternative way of appearing to the outside world. If you're wearing a mask in your dream, then you may feel that, in your waking life, you are hiding an aspect of your personality. If you are surrounded by people wearing masks, then perhaps you feel that the people around you are alienating, unnerving, and "not being themselves." You might want to consider if this is really an environment that you want to spend more time in.

MASTURBATION

One of those sexual taboos that most people prefer to keep behind closed doors, masturbation is now considered to be a normal practice. Dreaming of masturbation means that there are some things that you need to bring out in the open (although we don't suggest that you carry out the singular feature of your dream in a public place).

MAYPOLE

The maypole itself is a phallic symbol of fertility, used in particular during the May Day revels that were a throwback to the much earlier pre Christian celebration of Beltane. Complex patterns were woven in ribbon which extended from the top of the pole—girls danced in a counter-clockwise pattern, and the boys went clockwise, in the direction of the Sun. If you dream that you're participating in this dance, then the world is your oyster. It could also indicate that you have an active, healthy sex life. If you dream that you're merely observing it, then perhaps you lack confidence, and this lack of confidence might be in reference to your sensual life.

MAZE (*See* Labyrinth)

MEAT

Dreaming about meat if you're a vegetarian can be pretty horrific, but it might have to do with the need for guilty pleasures. Dreaming about eating human meat is also not as uncommon a dream as you might think, and the dream is telling you to use all resources necessary to get what you need. If you're eating raw meat, this could be to do with needing to find the animal side of your nature, or it could be that there's something in your waking life that you find repugnant and, figuratively speaking, "hard to swallow." If, on the other hand, the meat is tender and juicy and you're not a vegetarian, then it's likely that you're thinking about "feeding" the inner you—whatever that is!

ANXIETY DREAMS

Although in an ideal world we're meant to awaken from our eight hours of sleep feeling refreshed and rejuvenated, sometimes our sleep is disturbed and we feel as though we've spent those hours in a boxing ring. You know those nights—when you eventually get to sleep and fall into a deep slumber just an hour or so before you need to get up.

Chances are you've been having anxiety dreams. Don't worry, the dreams themselves are not the problem; they're simply the way that your subconscious mind reflects (and frequently exaggerates) the cares of your everyday working life. The bigger problem is the sleeplessness they can cause, which in itself can exacerbate those worries.

There are, however, ways to allay those dreams.

The first is to make a list of what your worries are and look at this list in the cold, clear light of day. Chances are that things are not as bad as you think, and you can start to work on your problems immediately and with clear focus.

Second, lay off heavy indigestible foods before bedtime. Just have a light snack; chamomile tea induces relaxation and lettuce is a soporific. Have a lettuce sandwich.

Third, spend a little time every day doing some deep, relaxed breathing. If you can add in a little meditation to the breathing exercise, then that would be even better.

If you do find yourself plagued with anxiety dreams despite these measures, don't lie tossing and turning. Get up and do something else for a short while; read a book or watch some stupid TV. Making lists of worries helps. You should find that sleep comes more easily if you stop resisting your sleepless state.

MECHANICS (MECHANICAL OBJECTS) *(See Machines)*

MEDAL

Dreams about giving or receiving medals, as well as other awards, is all about acknowledging and accepting praise for events and achievements in your waking life. Enjoy!

MEDICINE

They used to say that unless medicine tastes nasty, then it won't do your body any good. This isn't often the case these days, but in general we do have a tendency to believe that where there's no pain, there's no gain. So to dream that you're taking medicine means that there's something going on in your life that will undoubtedly get worse before it gets better. Don't worry; the tide will soon turn.

MEETING

Unless you're having one of those hideous dreams that simply replicate your working day, then dreaming about being in a meeting means that you might need to look to others for assistance with a certain project in your waking life. Two heads are better than one, and four can be better than two—if they're the right heads, that is! Don't be afraid to ask for help.

MEGAPHONE

If someone is speaking to you through a megaphone in your dream, then listen carefully. This might be your subconscious mind using a ploy to grab your attention. If you, on the other hand, are the one wielding the megaphone, then you need to make yourself heard in your waking life.

MELT

The process of melting is almost alchemical; a substance transforming into another state of being. The same applies to us; we change and our circumstances change, subtly, often without us realizing it. We also melt into love; is this what's happening to you? If you see someone you know melting, how do you feel about this? If you're frightened, then you're having an anxiety dream. If you dream that you are melting, then some aspect of your life is changing; it's even possible that you're losing a lot of weight!

MEMORIAL

Those of a spiritualist persuasion would say that a memorial dream is really a deceased loved one attempting to make contact with you. However, it is also possible that you are being reminded of someone—or something—that is very far from dead. This might be a long-lost friend; a "memorial" after all is about "remembering." There may be other clues in your dream as to who or what this is; be observant.

MERMAID

The mermaid used to be a symbol that indicated a brothel, or a place where sex could be bought for money. Though the mermaid cannot procreate, she is a profoundly sexual image—the ultimate in beguiling femininity. If you dream that you are a mermaid, your sensual side is making itself present and you are irresistibly attractive to the opposite sex—but with a certain distance. To dream that you see or meet a mermaid

means that you are close to attaining an object of desire. Play it cool.

MICE

Mice might be small, but they are more powerful than we sometimes give them credit for. Elephants, for example, are legendarily afraid of mice. And in *The Hitchhikers' Guide to the Galaxy*, writer Douglas Adams has mice as the real Masters of the Universe. A tiny mouse is a terrifying prospect to many people, but to dream of one is to realize your own hidden powers that others may also be unaware of.

MICROSCOPE

(*See* **Magnifying Glass**)

MILK

Milk is a symbol of the mother, nourishment, and goodness. Nevertheless, however, there's a cloying aspect to milk, and to dream of the stuff might mean that you're feeling somewhat overwhelmed by someone's attention. A little of what's good for you is great, but too much can make you sick. Spilled milk is certainly no disaster in real life, but to dream of spilled milk means that there's something not right in your life that you need to fix; there's a strong possibility that this is your relationship with your mother, your grandmother, or your mother-in-law.

MIME (See Deaf)

MINE

Mines run deep, and so does your subconscious mind. The hole that Alice fell down to find her wonderland was a kind of mineshaft; at the bottom of it, a whole realm of unexpected possibilities open up for her. Mines also hide unexpected treasure like diamonds or coal. Your mine dream is preparing you to unexpect the expected, both in your inner world and in the outer one. It's also a reminder that light can be found in every darkness.

MIRROR

*Aha...*a mirror is a very interesting dream symbol. If you're looking into a mirror in your dream, this can alert you to **Lucid Dreaming** (*see* page 156), since it's in a mirror that your conscious and subconscious minds meet.

Dreaming of a mirror is a very clear message that you need to look to yourself for the answers you're seeking; but first you need to define what the question is. If you're looking into a mirror and you see something or someone else reflected back at you, then this means that a surprise awaits you in your waking life.

How the mirror manifests itself is also well worth bearing in mind; it could appear as "normal," or it may be a reflective surface such as a sheet of metal, a lake, or a shiny object. If you see reflections in the shiny surface of a car, for example, then you need to take a journey to find something that you need. In real life, a broken or shattered mirror is the subject of superstitious belief that seven years' bad luck will follow. To dream of a broken mirror doesn't indicate a period of bad luck, but it might be an indicator that something in your own life is "shattered."

MISTLETOE

Sacred to the Druids, mistletoe was cut from its host tree with a golden scythe and never allowed to touch the ground. We might treat mistletoe with less reverence in general these days, but nevertheless the old beliefs about the plant die hard. The mistletoe is best known today, of course, for its ability to get you a kiss from someone while standing under it. To dream of mistletoe is an indication that you need to let go of your inhibitions.

MODEL

A model of anything at all represents an idealized state. So if you dream of a model, then you might be striving for something in your own life that's "model," and you're feeling anxious that you won't be able to achieve such perfection. Don't worry about it. There's no such thing.

MOHAWK

The mohawk haircut was adopted by the punk fraternity as a symbol of rebellion and is a fine example of how hair can define our tribal status.

To dream that you have a mohawk hairstyle indicates that you are not as rebellious in your waking life as you feel inside. Be yourself! (See also **Native American**.)

MONEY

Hard cash; when you think about it, it's not worth anything except for what we can buy with it. In many ways, money is one of the greatest illusions we ever invented though to most of us, it's an essential commodity. Symbolically speaking, money represents the material world. Seeing it in a dream could mean that you're attaching too much importance to it in your everyday life. Dreaming about money troubles is an anxiety dream. You need to think more laterally and pinpoint exactly what it is that you're anxious about.

MONK

Monks represent the spiritual aspect; but, this being *Freaky Dreams* after all, monks can also be a bit weird and creepy. To the layperson it might seem as though they cut themselves off from the outside world, and any sort of extreme can lead to weirdness unless

the monk is particularly well-adjusted. Asceticism is all very well, but it's not for everyone. The world of silent contemplation has a lot to offer, but then so does the one of wild parties and sensual desires. There's room for both in your life. If you dream of a monk, then you are thinking about seeking help from someone that you consider has a strong spiritual side.

MONKEY

Cute, funny, cheeky, agile—there are a lot of endearing aspects to monkeys and chimps, and they can also be kind of mischievous, with their leering grins and unexpected appearances. Beware the friendly monkey in your dream and in your life. He's very likely to be up to no good.

MOON

Symbolic of timeless and mysterious female energies, the moon in your dream denotes occult powers, moodiness, and secrets. If the moon is new, just a slivered crescent, expect new opportunities to arise for you very soon. If the moon is full, you need to watch out for hairs sprouting on the backs of your hands and inexplicable bouts of forgetfulness. Only joking... to dream of a full moon means that a project or idea you've been working on is about to reach fruition. If you dream that there's an eclipse of the moon, then you're anxious about something going badly wrong in your waking life. Face up to whatever it is and see if you can avert the impending disaster.

MOSAIC (*See* Jigsaw puzzles)

MOSQUE

To dream of any place of worship depends on which faith, if any, you belong to. If you are a Muslim, then the mosque dream is a clear reminder of your spiritual path. If you are not a Muslim, the dream tells you that there are many different ways to walk the same path. Revel in the mystic exoticism of an alternative way.

MOTH

Like butterflies, moths represent spirits. But because of their nocturnal habits, moths remind us more of spirits of the dead, and these tend to have a scarier association. Because moths live in dark places and appear at night, we associate them with the unknown. Their propensity for munching away at valuable fabrics also attaches them to the idea of decay and rot. A moth dream could indicate that you're harboring dark secrets that need to see the light of day or else they could destroy you.

MOTHER

What a mother actually is in terms of symbolism, and how your own mother presents herself to you, are not necessarily cut from the same cloth. To see a universal mother archetype in a dream means that you might be missing some of that motherly love in your real life. If you see your own mother, this dream is often associated with feelings of guilt. If it's not time to give her a call, then you need to consider your recent actions to see what's been making you feel guilty.

RECURRING DREAMS

As the name implies, a recurring dream is a dream which comes along more than once, sometimes reappearing at certain times through the life of the dreamer; sometimes the recurrent dream happens only a handful of times and then simply disappears.

If the dream is a lovely one, then it's fine to enjoy it. But if it's disturbing, or even something approaching a nightmare, you'll probably want to get rid of it. Here are some tips to stopping a recurring dream in its tracks:

- **Try to understand the dream; analyze what it means to you, and then use the A to Z entries in this book to learn about the symbolism of some of the objects in your dream.**
- **Appreciate that your subconscious mind is making great efforts to get you to understand something.**
- **Talk to that subconscious mind.**
- **Politely.**
- **Look for any aspect of the dream that might, if you looked at them in a different way, prove enjoyable or entertaining.**
- **Make detailed notes of the content of your recurring dream every time you have it. Watch out for subtle changes or nuances.**
- **Consider whether there are connecting patterns in your waking life that might cause a flare-up of the dream.**
- **Sometimes recurring dreams—even the nightmare kind—can prove useful in understanding who you are. Enjoy the experience as much as you can.**

MOUNTAINS

Traditionally places of spiritual enlightenment where we communicate with the gods, it's no coincidence that Moses received the Ten Commandments at the top of a mountain. If you are looking at mountains in your dream, then you are aware of the spiritual quest that your life holds. If you are climbing the mountain, then you're on your way to accomplishing great things, but you know that it's not always as easy as it seems. If you're at the top of the mountain in your dream, then you have made a great achievement in your waking life, and your subconscious is telling you to be proud of yourself. If you are lost on a mountain, then your dream is reflecting your jumbled state of mind regarding that spiritual quest. Play with your dreams for a few days to find out how you can "find your way" again.

MULE

Mules are notoriously stubborn, so to dream of one could mean that there is someone or something in your life that is as equally stubborn, something that refuses to go away. However, mules are also strong and useful, and these qualities, as well as that stubbornness, can be used to advantage if you learn how to handle them.

MURDER

If you are the murderer in the dream, then this means you have to effectively "murder" something in your life that you no longer need. This might be represented by an actual person, but don't worry, it's likely to be a particular quality embodied by the person that you need to rid from your life—not the actual person. However, murder is also liable to be accompanied by a deal of guilt. This feeling of guilt and/ or responsibility might be preventing you from enacting the "murder" in real life. Have a long hard think about which is more important; your own well being and state of mind, or the "thing" which your mind understands has to be eliminated?

FAMOUS FREAKY DREAMERS
THE ROLLING STONE

There are some occasions in which an idea in a dream ejects itself from the subconscious mind straight into the conscious one with no seeming effort required. This happened to Keith Richards. His particular slice of subconscious serendipity became one of the most famous rock and roll songs on the planet, "Satisfaction."

Here's how Keith describes the incident in his autobiography, *Life*:

Then came "Satisfaction," the track that launched us into global fame. I was between girlfriends at the time...Hence maybe the mood of the song. I wrote "Satisfaction" in my sleep. I had no idea I'd written it, it's only thank God for the little Phillips cassette player. The miracle being that I looked at the cassette player that morning and I knew I'd put a brand-new tape in the previous night, and I saw it was at the end. Then I pushed "rewind" and there was "Satisfaction"...And forty minutes of me snoring.

MUSEUM

A museum dream is like a "container" dream, in other words, the container (museum, in this case) represents you. A museum houses rare and precious objects, many of them antiques. These precious objects represent your inherent skills and qualities, those you have been born with and those that you have acquired through diligence and hard work. The dream is a reminder that it's time to open those museum doors and let in the public.

MUSICAL INSTRUMENTS

There are entries listed under specific instruments, but in general, these are all about harmony. If you are playing an instrument solo, then the dream indicates that you need to make your voice heard a little more frequently in your waking life. If you are playing in an orchestra, then you need to concentrate on teamwork. Generally speaking, musical instrument dreams are good dreams to have.

MUSTACHE (See Beard)

NAILS

Metal nails or fingernails? Let's take the metal type first.

Nails fix things into place. Firmly. There's finality about something that's nailed in, and this dream could be suggesting that you need to nail shut a particular situation in your life.

Fingernails, on the other hand, tell us an awful lot about the state of our health. And they still give us clues as to a person's status. In times gone by, long nails were the mark of someone who didn't have to do manual labor in order to make a living. Today, long and garishly painted nails tend to be enjoyed by those with no taste and lots of time to spare. What type of nails appeared in your dream? If the latter, maybe there are certain issues that you have been avoiding.

NAME

If you see your name written, or hear it called in your dream, then you're very much in touch with your own self and your own identity. Such an encounter can also presage a lucid dream episode, so be alert. To dream that you forget the name of someone you know very

well is related to anxiety in waking life. Breathe, walk tall, relax, and don't sweat the small stuff.

NATIVE AMERICAN

Many spirit guides seem to come in the guise of a Native American Indian. The Native American in your dreams speaks of your spiritual side and the connection with the natural world in all its forms. Don't ignore this side of yourself. Spookily, such dreams frequently seem to have backup in synchronicitous events in everyday waking life.

NAVEL

The navel represents the center, as well as the place of connection with the mother, via the umbilical cord. You are seeking to "ground" yourself and understand your connection with the world; this is precisely why we use the term "navel gazing" to describe someone involved in an intense quest to discover themselves. Don't take life too seriously—you're as likely to attain self-comprehension by having fun and involving yourself with the world as by removing yourself from it.

NAZI

Any sort of fascist pretender speaks of an alienating force that cannot and will not be reasoned with—and an evil force to boot. What person or situation in your waking life has such Nazi qualities, and what can you do to blow them apart?

NECK

Symbolically, the neck is a sort of bridge between the head (mind) and the body. So an emphasis on the neck in a dream signifies the need for a greater connection between the two. You might find this in meditation or a similar discipline.

NECKLACE

Jewelry aside, the necklace specifically represents erotic desires, which have as much to do with the mind as with the body. Sexual arousal happens in both. It's no accident that the necklace was a favored gift for mistresses.

NECTAR

There's sweetness in little things whose cost cannot be related to monetary value alone. Go out and find them.

NEEDLE

A needle is an instrument of union, used to join two halves together. But to "needle" someone means to nag them about something. It's possible that both aspects of this dream bear relevance for you.

NEST

A "container" dream, the nest symbolizes comfort and coziness. But in reality, the nest is only really comfortable if you're a bird. Is your current lifestyle entirely appropriate or do you maybe need to downsize?

There's no need to compromise on comfort, simply change your expectations instead. Get used to twigs.

NEWSPAPER

Newspapers do give us the news, but the paper in your dream might have a subliminal message of "news" that is specifically aimed at you. Pay close attention to any particular headlines, especially those that might appear to be in some kind of code. Dreams often communicate in roundabout ways.

NIGHTMARE

(*See* **What Exactly is a Nightmare?** opposite.)

NIGHTTIME

A dream that takes place in the hours of darkness speaks even more of subconscious messages than those that take place in the daytime. Not to say that these dreams are more valid—it's just that they are liable to be more poignant and noticeable. They are full of symbols, ideas, and concepts that want to attract your attention. For example, to dream of white horses at night enhances the meaning of the horses (*See* **Horse**).

NOOSE

Implies restrictions, situations that are holding you back, and frustrations that make you feel you are being strangled. If the noose is actually around your neck, then you need to act swiftly, since it's in your power alone to change the situation. If you are the hangman, then you need to radically alter your behavior toward the people around you.

NORTHERN LIGHTS

If you actually witness the shifting and changing iridescent, nocturnal, rainbow formations of the Northern Lights in your dream, then you could be about to gain full lucidity, especially if you've never actually experienced them in real life. Either that, or astral travel. Prepare for liftoff!

NOSE

Things could be more obvious, easier, and simpler than you think if they are right under your nose, figuratively speaking. Otherwise, perhaps you're detecting something or sniffing something out, or you have detected an unusual smell. It could be that the nose in a dream represents you interfering

WHAT EXACTLY IS A NIGHTMARE?

It's a "bad" dream, right? Technically speaking, a nightmare is a dream that elicits a reaction of horror, terror, fear, or all three, in the dreamer. Nightmares can be so bad that sometimes it's hard to shake off that feeling of horror, and it's often difficult to get back to sleep after one. You need to read a funny book or watch some stupid late night TV to dispel the nastiness. Sometimes, if the unfortunate dreamer experiences a series of nightmares night after night, he or she might even try to avoid going to sleep at all. This can lead to insomnia, and lack of sleep will only serve to exacerbate anxiety.

Nightmares are more common than you might think; scientific studies tell us that roughly three quarters of all dreams contain the sort of subject matter that transforms those dreams into nightmares. One of the worst kinds of nightmares occurs when something horrendous has happened to a person in real life, and the individual is forced to endure aspects of it replaying over and over again during sleeping hours.

But where does the word "nightmare" come from? The "mare" part of the word has its origins in the Old English *maere*, meaning a malicious spirit, specifically an incubus or possibly a goblin. In fact, the ancient Dutch word for "goblin" is *mare*, and the Icelandic, *mara*, means "incubus". An incubus is a poisonous female entity that legendarily sits on the sleeper, suffocating him and draining his energy, vampire-like. In the sixteenth century, the word "nightmare" was used to describe a "bad dream caused by an incubus". In later years, we've largely forgotten about the supernatural aspect of a bad dream, which is probably just as well. The very thought of an evil spirit crushing your ribs and sucking away your bodily energies is enough to give anyone nightmares.

FAMOUS FREAKY DREAMERS
YESTERDAY

Paul McCartney is one of the most famous and successful singer/songwriters of all time, and one of his best-loved songs was inspired by a dream.

"Yesterday," written in 1965, is one of the most covered songs of all times and while it's impossible to count just how many times the song has been broadcast or performed, the official body that logs such information estimates seven million plays of the song in the twentieth century. And this song came to McCartney in a dream. It happened during the filming of the Beatles' movie, *Help*. Paul was sleeping in a small attic room in London's Wimpole Street. Here's what happened, in his own words:

I woke up with a lovely tune in my head. I thought, "That's great, I wonder what that is?" There was an upright piano next to me, to the right of the bed by the window. I got out of bed, sat at the piano, found G, found F sharp minor 7th—and that leads you through then to B to E minor, and finally back to E. It all leads forward logically. I liked the melody a lot, but because I'd dreamed it, I couldn't believe I'd written it. I thought, "No, I've never written anything like this before." But I had the tune, which was the most magic thing!

What's really interesting here is McCartney's sense of disbelief that he could have written such a fully-formed piece of music. It's almost as though the ideas that strike us during the dream-state have the power to circumnavigate our busy egos. It's not surprising that so many musicians, writers, artists, and other creatives are into meditation, too, since this can also help bring the subconscious mind to the fore.

in someone else's business, or they're messing around in yours.

NOTES

Read them carefully, if you can; this could be an oblique message from your subconscious. Actual musical notes—those little black dots—represent the first seven letters of the alphabet (a to g). If you are able to read these black dots, then it could be they're spelling out a message for you.

NUDITY

(*See* **Nakedness** on page 81)

NUMBERS

Numbers are a way of weighing and measuring things, as well as handy tools of calculation. If you dream of numbers that don't add up, then things similarly fail to "add up" in your waking life and you may be worried about your bank balance. There's only one person who can balance those metaphorical books...

NUN *(See* **Monk***)*

Except replace the word "male" with "female" and add in "repressed sexuality."

NURSE

There are two aspects to the nurse in your dreams. Firstly, the obvious one; healing, medicine, bedpans, and kindness. The second is the sort that has erotic connotations. So, depending on the context in which your dream nurse appears, your dream is telling you that you need a particular kind of healing.

NUTCRACKER

"Nuts" are a euphemism for a particular part of the male anatomy. If you're a man and you're dreaming of nutcrackers, then it's likely that this particular part of your own anatomy is being squeezed. Metaphorically speaking.

OAK

Trees have a dream symbolism all of their own, but the oak is so important as a symbol of strength, longevity, and solidarity that it deserves a mention of its own. However, if you dream that you are chopping down an oak, beware that you might be destroying something valuable in your everyday life.

OASIS

You are longing for something so much that it's becoming unhealthy. Define what that thing is and go and get it in real life.

OBELISK

A hard, unmoving, solid, phallic shape, pointing skyward. To dream of an obelisk means that you may be deprived of physical affection.

OBITUARY

Any kind of written material in a dream can have a direct message. If you're reading an obituary, then some out-of-date and unnecessary aspect of your life have "died." Congratulations!

OBSERVATORY

If in your dream you are standing in an observatory, then you are in the enviable position of being able to take an objective look at the landscape of your own life. What you see in that landscape merits further investigation, but the general outlook is very good indeed, because being in the observatory implies understanding and control.

OCEAN

Any body of water represents the feminine element— your moods, and emotions. So the state of the ocean paints your own internal picture. For example, if the waters are choppy and tumultuous, then the state of your emotions are similarly fraught. If the ocean is calm and serene, then so, too, are your internal "waters."

OCTOPUS

Do you feel restricted, strangled by the tentacles of officialdom or similar? The octopus in your dream reflects your life experience right now.

OFFICE

If you work in an office, to spend time dreaming about it implies anxiety and an unhealthy obsession with work. Think about the balance of your life and try to improve matters. If you don't work in an office, then perhaps your life is in need of a little more organization.

OFFICIAL

If you dream of anyone in a uniform that appears to have an official capacity, it could be that you feel in need of some guidance and control in your life. You may even be seeking more authority and direction. Either that or you have an unfulfilled fetish about epaulettes, etc.

OIL

A calming, soothing influence, to dream of oil implies that you need this soothing influence in your life.

OLIVES

Any dream of eating relates to spiritual enrichment, but the olive deserves a mention all of its own. It symbolizes healthiness, longevity, contentment, and a certain level of exotica. Are these things a part of your life or do you feel that you're missing them?

OLYMPIC CIRCLES

The five linked circles of the famous Olympic logo denote unity. It may be that the number five is significant to you: five friends, five members of a family, five workmates. Whatever it is, the dream tells you that these five elements are working harmoniously together.

OMELET

You can't make an omelet without breaking eggs. This dream shows the culmination of a lot of hard work or an idea that has worked and is becoming reality. You have made sacrifices, but they've been worth it. Congratulations!

ONION

"The World is just a great big onion…" or so the words of the song by Ashford and Simpson go. The dream onion reflects the lyrics of this song; there are many layers to be peeled away before we get to the true nature of anything. Life itself is an onion, but there's no need to cry as you dissect it.

OPERATION

If you are a surgeon in your dream, it might be that you have a friend that needs to have something "removed." Or you yourself might be on an operating table, about to go under the knife. This dream is about taking things away or having them taken away. Think about what situation this reflects in your waking life.

OPIUM

If you dream that you are enjoying the delights of an opium den, then you are wishing, in your everyday life, to expand your consciousness. Opium may not be the strictly legal way to do it, but you are determined to explore other realms. Have fun and stay safe.

ORCHARD

The ultimate heavenly ideal, the orchard symbolizes prosperity, happiness, and longevity. Your dream is telling you that all these things are within your grasp. It could even be that you're looking forward to reaping the fruit of your labors in some way.

ORCHIDS

Flowers have a particular symbolism, but orchids deserve a mention all of their own since they carry deep sexual connotations. Even the word "orchid" derives from the Greek word for "testicles." To dream of orchids means that you need to liberate your sensual, sexual side.

ORGY

This sort of dream can be quite disturbing, no matter what your attitude toward sex. It could be that you feel sexually threatened in some way, in your waking life, or that you are being pressured into something that you'd rather not be a part of. If the dream recurs, you might want to seek therapy. Then again, many people enjoy orgies as a harmless and regular part of their sexual lives or fantasy lives, and you could, too. Otherwise, the orgy dream brings you face to face with unspoken sexual desires that you may or may not want to pursue in your waking life.

ORIGAMI

In moments of clarity, we see that life unfolds away from us like a piece of backward origami; the shape of it revealed only briefly. To dream of origami is to understand the perfection and precision of the final shape we're making, even if we don't know what that shape is at the time we're making it.

OSTRICH

Big, fluffy birds that can't fly and stick their head in the sand because they want to ignore stuff. If that's your perception of an ostrich, it's probably telling you to start paying attention to a situation.

OUIJA BOARD

The Ouija board, also known as a "planchette," was once a popular way for people to try to contact disembodied spirits, apparently often with spectacularly frightening results. Whatever the efficacy of such a device, the Ouija is another way of communication and it may be possible that your subconscious mind uses it as a way of telling you something.

Otherwise, it could be to do with you needing to use more straightforward methods of communication in your everyday life, and perhaps it's better to concentrate on the living rather than the dead.

OWL

The owl merits an entry all of its own. Its nocturnal habits mean that the owl has long been regarded as having access to hidden information and secret knowledge—wisdom in many areas, but especially in the occult. To dream of an owl often means that something is about to be revealed to you, but it could be in an unexpected or obtuse sort of way. This kind of dream is a reminder to keep your senses alert.

OYSTER

Long considered an aphrodisiac, there are inevitable sexual connotations in a dream about oysters. The shape and texture of the oyster reeks of eroticism and illicit pleasures, and this dream tells you that you are longing for such stimulus in your everyday life. It's up to you to find that stimulus.

PACKING

In your dream you might be packing physical objects, but in real life it could well be situations and emotions that you're putting into boxes. We pack things away for future use—whether we're putting the things in the attic or taking them on vacation. Ask yourself whether or not you actually still need the stuff you're packing away.

PAGE

You need to observe, if you can, what sort of book the page belongs to, and if it's blank or full of text, or if you're turning the page backward or forward. If it's old, tired, and tatty, you need to have a long, hard look at all the things you ought to be changing in your life.

PAINT (PAINTING)

Whichever way paint is being used in your dream (whether to paint pictures or to cover walls), it's good and implies a conscious desire to freshen and brighten your life and your environment. If you find yourself splashing paint around à la Jackson Pollock, be aware that your life is full of frustrations that you want to get rid of in drastic ways. If you're painting it black, it's possible that you are full of dark thoughts.

PALACE

A palace in your dreams represents aspirations and the infinite possibilities that could potentially appear in your life. Unless, of course, you already live in one, in which case you're a very lucky person.

PALMS

Traditionally, the palms of the hands both foretell and designate the fate of their owner. If you are looking at palms in your dream, then you are being given information in a roundabout way. Expect some kind of enlightenment in the very near future.

PAN

Do we mean mundane skillet pans or the glamorous, great god, Pan? Here at Freaky Dreams Central, we prefer the more exotic subject matter. To dream of the mighty-horned god is to understand the animal part of your nature—the instinctive, intuitive you that encourages you to live your life as a work of art, outside of the usual conventions of polite society. Pan encourages you to walk on the wild side. A skillet pan, on the other hand, is symbolic of domesticity, nurturing, and the feeding of your family and friends. Perhaps you need to make more time for this sort of thing in your waking life.

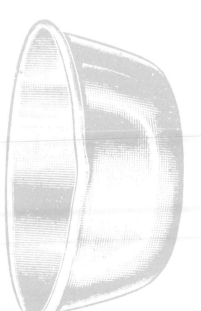

PAPERWORK

A symbol of your responsibilities and worries, if you are tackling paperwork in your dream, you could be anxious about things in your waking life, and it's possible that you are ignoring these anxieties.

PARACHUTE

Dreaming of a parachute implies that you are being looked after. Take risks, or take that great leap into the unknown, and you will find that these leaps of faith will pay off. If you dream that your parachute fails, however, you need to put in a little more work and preparation before you make any drastic moves.

PARENTS

A parent or parents represent the mature, protective aspects of yourself. If you dream that your parents are dead, when in real life they are alive, then you are undergoing a rapid phase of maturity; it's possible that this is the time that you are coming close to starting a family of your own.

PARK

Any sort of garden or other outside area represents your spiritual life. So the sort of park it is, and the state of it, will inform you as to the meaning of the dream. Your own feeling within the context of the park will also reveal a great deal. If you are in the park at nighttime, then you are facing what Jung called the "shadow" side of yourself. This is good and marks a significant period of self-understanding and spiritual growth.

PARROT

Parrots are known for their talent for imitation. Perhaps you feel that someone is copying you or stealing your ideas, for example. Relax about it and remember that imitation is apparently the sincerest form of flattery.

PASSPORT

What are you waiting for? Book a flight to somewhere lovely and make that dream come true! Aside from this, the passport symbolizes your own identity and the places that you've traveled, metaphorically speaking. Its appearance in your dream might mean that you are taking stock, considering how far you have come—or how far you'd like to go.

PAST TIMES

If you dream vividly of past events in your own life, then this means that your subconscious mind is helping you process whatever happened. If this is at all painful, then sit with it, as you need to come to terms with past events. If you dream vividly of past events in the lives of others, then it is likely that these happenings have a bearing on your life, too, which perhaps you hadn't realized in your waking life. Consider them again in the light of your dream.

PEARL

Pearls represent something precious and rare...wisdom, purity, and elegance. If your dream shows a string of broken pearls, then you might feel that you are compromising your principles somehow. If you dream of finding a pearl, then you are discovering the beauty that's inside of you.

PEN (PENCIL)

If you are writing something in your dream, try to read what you have written. If it's the writing implement alone that appears in your dream, then this might suggest that there's something you need to write for your own peace of mind. The fancier the writing implement, the more important the message.

PEACH

Sensual pleasures, fun, and enjoyment are embodied by the peach in a dream. If these are missing in your life, then only you can solve this dilemma. Incidentally, in the East the peach stone is a symbol of good luck and longevity.

PEACOCK

Not only symbolic of love, the peacock has the more unfortunate allusions of pride and arrogance. Is your behavior peacocklike, or maybe someone you know is acting in such a way? Enjoy the beauty and put any annoyances to one side.

PENGUIN

How is the penguin different from other birds? The obvious answer is that the penguin cannot fly. It is possible that you're feeling frustrated or held back by what you perceive to be the actions of others. Like the colors of the penguin, some things in life really are black and white. You know what the truth is and you know what works. Follow what's under your nose, and be aware that you don't always need wings.

PERISCOPE

You need to look at things in a different way, to gain a new perspective on a frustrating old situation. But you might have to take roundabout ways to do this. The operable part of the periscope is the mirror, so bear that in mind and realize that there are many different angles on any situation and lots of different ways of looking at things.

PHONE

Dreaming of a phone indicates communication of some kind. You may be lucky enough to have a phone conversation in your dream; if so, try to remember the contents, as this could be a very direct communication with your subconscious mind.

PHOTO

Photographs in your dreams represent moments past and memories. The photos you tend to dream about are generally happy moments and could mean that you are longing for a return to these happy times.

PILGRIMAGE

A pilgrimage represents the journey of your life, whether or not you regard yourself as "spiritual." Your position or progress within your dream pilgrimage will tell you what you need to know. Traditionally, a pilgrimage is a tough journey, but getting through its hardships gives a great feeling of achievement. Perhaps you're going through a tough time right now and need a reminder of the bigger picture.

PINEAPPLE

A prickly and difficult exterior protects the sweet and tasty center of a pineapple. This is most probably a dream about yourself or someone that you're interested in.

PIPE

Smoking a pipe in your dream means that you are gaining wisdom and knowledge. It also suggests a period

FAMOUS FREAKY DREAMERS
JEKYLL AND HYDE

Robert Louis Stevenson, in his relatively short life that ran from 1850—1894, is among an illustrious number of writers that ascribe their literary inventions to dream inspirations. One of the most famous of these is *The Strange Case of Dr. Jekyll and Mr. Hyde*, the tale of a man who suffers from an extreme character alteration that takes him from nice to nasty in a matter of seconds. Stevenson took only 10 weeks to complete the story, including printing it, after the initial dream. Here's what he said at the time:

For two days I went about racking my brains for a plot of any sort; and on the second night I dreamed the scene at the window, and a scene afterward split in two, in which Hyde, pursued for some crime, took the powder and underwent the change in the presence of his pursuers.

Stevenson, though, had made the early discovery that his dreamscapes offered a whole world of wonder and entertainment, and trained himself to "climb back into" dreams on consecutive evenings, pursuing the story. This talent repaid him very richly.

FAMOUS FREAKY DREAMERS
THE NOBEL PRIZE WINNER

Dr. Otto Loewi (1873—1961) had every right to say "Most so called 'intuitive' discoveries are such associations made in the subconscious." This is precisely how he discovered conclusively that nerve impulses are chemically transmitted, as opposed to electrically, as had previously been believed. Here's how he describes his own "intuitive discovery:"

The night before Easter Sunday of that year I awoke, turned on the light, and jotted down a few notes on a tiny slip of paper. Then I fell asleep again. It occurred to me at 6 o'clock in the morning that during the night I had written down something most important, but I was unable to decipher the scrawl. The next night, at 3 o'clock, the idea returned. It was the design of an experiment to determine whether or not the hypothesis of chemical transmission that I had uttered 17 years ago was correct. I got up immediately, went to the laboratory, and performed a single experiment on a frog's heart according to the nocturnal design.

It's worth noting that Loewi had had his suspicions about chemical impulses for the previous 17 years. Such a dream would have meant nothing to anyone who didn't have expertise in the area, but it would take another ten years of hard work and experiments before he won the Nobel Prize in 1936.

of relaxed harmony and enlarged perspective in your life. Marvelous!

PIRATE

A pirate represents anything that's illicit or forbidden. Despite the pirate being a criminal and an outlaw, there can also be something wonderfully exotic, naughty, and fun about a pirate in your dreams. Perhaps a little of what you fancy might do you good?

PLANTS

Plants symbolize the earthy side of human nature. A dream of lush jungle vegetation is a reminder of your wild side; if your dream is of an orderly garden full of pruned roses, trained trees, and sculpted bushes, then perhaps you're a little repressed.

PLUMBING

If you notice faulty plumbing in your dream, this could be a warning to get yourself checked out by a doctor. Your subconscious mind knows more about your health than you might give it credit for.

POCKET

A pocket in your dreams represents a part of you that is private. If it is actually empty, then it's time for you to learn that new skill you're interested in. Whatever you find in your pocket represents a talent that it's time to use in public.

POMEGRANATE

Representing fertility and creativity, as well as slightly illicit sensual pleasures, dreaming of a pomegranate might mean that your waking life is bereft of such joys. Only you can change this.

POND (POOL)

Any body of water represents the state of your emotions. If the surface of the pond or pool in your dream is choppy and tumultuous, then so are those emotions. If the surface is calm and mirrorlike, then you, too, are in a serene and contemplative state.

PORCUPINE

The spines on the porcupine tell you that you might be feeling the need to protect yourself from the outside world. It could be in reaction to a particular situation, or it might be that you live your everyday life in a fearful state.

PRAYER

To dream that you are kneeling in prayer is to dream that you need to ask for help. The likelihood is that this help may need to come from a worldlier source than a divine power, but it's as good a place as any to start. You have the answers inside yourself in any case.

PRIEST

A trusted figure of authority, a priest in your dream will tell you what you need to know. It could be that he is behaving in an unexpected manner; this means that you should consider taking a lateral approach to a particular situation or problem.

PRISON

To be in a prison is to be trapped and can be a punishment for something that you may or may not be guilty of. But the prison cell of your dream might also reflect an aspect of your life that's making you feel trapped or which you feel punished by, whether or not you deserve it. To dream that you are in prison is another of the very common anxiety dreams, and if this dream is recurrent, then you really do need to look at the circumstances of your waking life that might be responsible for the "trapped" or "punished" feelings.

PROSTITUTE

To dream that you are a prostitute means that you feel you are compromising yourself in some way, and you should think about whether this compromise is really worth it. It doesn't necessarily need to be about sex, since we can "prostitute" ourselves in all sorts of ways. Essentially, prostitution signifies an exchange of moral values for material gain. If you dream that a friend of yours is a prostitute, then you should be aware that everyone has a hidden side.

PUMPKIN

The ultimate magical vegetable (that's really a fruit) that swells to enormous proportions in fairy stories and was even used as a vehicle by rags-to-riches heroine Cinderella. The appearance of a pumpkin in your dream tells you to never take ordinary, everyday things for granted.

PYRAMID

They're big, they're iconic, and they're mysterious. We are still not entirely sure how the pyramids were built, and we can't really comprehend the importance that the Egyptians attached to them. To dream of the pyramids means that there is an aspect of your own life that you are similarly mystified by, something that is looming and significant. This could either be a person or a situation. Try and gain new perspective to understand this "thing;" look at it with a different viewpoint.

QUAKER

Quakers might appear in your dream, or you may find yourself as a member of this spiritual group. If you are not a Quaker in everyday life, then you need to embrace some of the tranquility and gentle spiritual ideals of these people. Any way of exploring your neglected spiritual side has to be a good thing in general, and to dream of Quakers in particular might imply that you need to live a simpler, calmer life.

QUARANTINE

Being placed in quarantine is akin to being imprisoned, albeit for different reasons. This period of enforced removal from normal social interaction is disorienting and scary in a dream, but essential in making you take a look at your conscious situation. If you see that there are areas of your waking life that are "quarantined," then look with clarity at the reasons for this and make moves to improve matters.

QUARTZ CRYSTALS

The sparkling loveliness and longevity of quartz show resilience and beauty in your dreams. The color of the stone also has meaning; for example, pink could imply that there's love in your life, or green could signify new beginnings (*See Colors*). If the stone is murky, there might be parts of your life that you're not feeling too happy about. This might be to do with areas where you feel your integrity is being compromised.

QUEEN

Representing the epitome of femininity, the queen in your dream may also be an aspect of either yourself or your mother. However, the queen is also someone to be feared, often cruel and heartless—think of the Ice Queen, for example, or the Queen who regularly shouts, "Off with their heads!" in *Alice's Adventures in*

Wonderland. Whatever her nature, a Queen represents an aspect of yourself that you need to come to terms with.

QUESTIONS

If you find yourself asking questions in your dream, then take heed of an old adage that if you have the capacity for the question, then you have a similar capacity for its answer. If, however, others are asking you persistent questions, then you may feel that you are under pressure in your everyday life, overburdened with others' problems and issues.

QUICKSILVER

Also the name for mercury, implying ideas, fast thought processes, intelligence, and communication. Your dream implies that you are frustrated by the lack of these skills in those around you.

QUILT

To dream that you are making a quilt implies a project that needs to be tackled with care, diligence, and precision. If you are snuggled in quilts, then you are being comforted for a lack of material goods in your waking life. Waking from such a lovely dream might even make you feel bereft. Don't go back to sleep—instead, focus on making your waking life equally comfortable.

RABBIT

Generally a symbol of good luck, a rabbit in your dream is also a reminder of your own sexuality, since rabbits are remarkably keen procreators. Are you considering starting a family or about to undertake fertility treatment?

RACING

If you are observing a race, then it's likely that you're slightly out of touch and a little detached from the trajectory of your own life. If, on the other hand, you dream that you are running in a race, then your position among the other competitors will tell you much about your mental state. If you are right at the back and struggling to keep up, you're anxious about your career prospects. If you're ahead of the others, you could be equally anxious at the efforts you need to make to retain this leading position. It depends on your personal disposition.

RADIO

The subconscious mind tries to get messages to us in any way it can. If your dream involves a radio broadcast, then it's likely that the contents of the program will contain information that is important to you. If the signal is patchy, then you're not ready to receive such information, but don't turn off— do your best to tune in!

RAFT

This may seem like a precarious way to travel in the water, but rafts are the product of necessity and ingenuity. A dream about rafts indicates that you have such qualities in abundance and circumstances in your life might soon require you to prove this. You will be surprised at how effective a raft can actually be, despite the lack of choice you might sometimes have as to the direction it chooses to take.

RAILWAY STATION

An in-between place, you find yourself waiting at a railway station when you're on a journey. In your dreams, this could indicate a similar sort of holding pattern in your everyday life.

RAIN

If you find yourself in a relentless rainstorm, then it could well be that you are resisting certain changes that are sweeping into your life. Water represents the spiritual aspect, changes that need to be made for your own greater good, and this dream tells you to "go with the flow.".If the rain is a light shower, then you're slowly embracing the refreshing new mental attitudes that are becoming a part of your life.

RAINBOW

The rainbow is a strong symbol of hope, and you might even dream that you find the end of the rainbow and that legendary crock of gold that's said to be buried there. In your dream world, that crock of gold represents you and you are your own cache of gold. A wonderful moment of completion, contentment, and satisfaction is coming your way.

RAM

The symbol for the astrological sign of Aries, the ram is known to be sexually voracious, determined to the point of stubbornness, and more likely to use brute force than subtle reasoning. These qualities could be evident in yourself or in someone you know, or your dream could be telling you that these are qualities that would be useful in your life right now.

RATS

Although we often perceive rats to be scary creatures, spreading poison and disease, they are in fact incredibly intelligent and resourceful animals. If you are being attacked by rats, then perhaps you are neglecting this resourceful and resilient side of yourself. If you are afraid of the rats in your dream, then you need to ask yourself which aspect of your "inner rat" it is that you are afraid of...perhaps you're scared to show just how smart you are?

RAVEN

To dream of ravens is to dream of a powerful animal, known in traditions the world over to be intelligent, instinctive, spiritually aware, and a true messenger of the gods. This, despite their alarming appearance as black harbingers of doom, which might be another aspect of the raven in your dream. Watch these dream birds and hold their power within yourself despite any vestigial frightening appearance. Observe these powerful birds and listen to what they are telling you.

REBIRTH

We usually don't remember much about our first birth, but a rebirth of any kind is a painful process for many, involving throwing away old attitudes and rejecting obsolete belief systems. This takes courage, but your dream is telling you that not only is some kind of rebirth utterly necessary, but that you're ready to take whatever "pain" it is that comes with the "gain."

RECIPE

When a recipe features in your dream, it is never just about straightforward cooking. Take note of the ingredients; they could relate to qualities that you are not using in your waking life, or qualities you need to gain in order to make the cake that is your life.

REFLECTION (*See* **Mirror**)

REINCARNATION

If your belief system encompasses such a concept, then your dream could provide an important clue as to what's coming next for you. But we don't have to die in order to be reincarnated—we can change our jobs, our personalities, even our sex, and be reborn as someone else. Your dream is reminding you of this possibility.

REINDEER

The versatility of the reindeer is immense. It can live in the hardiest of surroundings, and its legendary magical powers and fly-drive capabilities are renowned. To dream of any animal is to know that you, too, possess its particular skills and attributes, so embrace your inner reindeer!

REPTILE

The reptilian brain that is a part of all human beings is the part that is responsible for the most basic of functions. To dream of the reptile is a reminder of this most essential, but primitive part of ourselves. Don't be afraid of it.

RICE

A basic foodstuff, to dream of eating rice means that you need to pay more attention to the most basic of your spiritual needs; take time to notice and take pleasure in the natural world that surrounds you.

RING

A symbol of eternity, the ring as a piece of jewelry bears particular significance depending on which finger it's worn on in your dreams. The index finger shows that you want to take control. The ring finger indicates a desire for union. The middle finger is about the balance that you need to find in your life. The little finger indicates sexual ambiguity, and the thumb means that you've lived this life once before. If it's a wedding or engagement ring, then perhaps this is something that you're thinking of or wishing for.

RIVER

Any body of water denotes the state of your emotions, and as a moving body of water, the river indicates change. You can't change the world, but you can change your mind and the way you think about things. Go with the flow of that dream river, observing its color, speed, and general nature to determine what it is you're feeling.

ROAD AND ROAD SIGNS

The road represents your journey through life; the road signs are the series of inner checks and balances that tell you where you are on your journey and what you need to do to get to where you want to be. If the road ahead of you is smooth, sleek and well kept, then you see your way through life as being equally easy at the moment. If the road is rough and bumpy, then your current "journey" is equally arduous. If the traffic is against you, then it's likely that you're perceiving obstacles and delays in your waking life; a smooth flow of vehicles implies the opposite.

ROBES

If you are wearing robes in your dream, then you would like to be in a position of some authority and are dissatisfied with your current situation in waking life, whether personal or work related.

ROCKET

To dream of a rocket signifies your ambitions and aspirations, and if it's zooming into the air, then it's likely that your ideas are taking off in a big way! If the rocket, however, fails to launch, then it's a sign that you need to go back to the drawing board on an idea that you've had.

ROOM

A "container" dream, the room represents an aspect of you, but is less daunting in size than an entire house. Observe the details in the room—if it is crammed full of clutter and difficult to navigate, you need to have a mental clear out. If the room is calm, elegant, and peaceful, then you're in an organized and settled frame of mind. If the room is upstairs, it relates to your "higher mind." If downstairs, it's relating to your subconscious.

ROSES

Although flowers have significance all of their own, roses are so important that they merit their own entry. Considered to be one of the most beautiful and iconic of flowers, observe the color of the rose and its condition. A tightly wrapped rosebud implies that you have secrets. An open, blowsy rose tells you that maybe you can be a little too open. If the rose in your dream carries a scent that you can actually smell, this is very rare and many would tell you that the spirit world is sending you a very special message.

RUBIES

Rubies stand for love, passion, and desire; they are also a symbol of spiritual riches. This dream is giving you the things that you feel you are missing in your waking life and should be a great source of comfort to you. Enjoy their beauty!

SACK

Any kind of bag or sack tends to represent the womb and signals a desire for a return to security and protection—an impossible dream, but think about what is happening in your life that might be making you crave this.

SADDLE

Dreaming of a saddle implies taking responsibility for your own life, and to be "in the saddle" is to be in control.

SAFE

Are you trying to crack a safe in your dream? If so, then you're trying to find inner strength and access talents that you know you have, even if they are well hidden. You need to gain confidence in yourself.

SAILING

Depending on the circumstances and the conditions that you're sailing in, if you're expertly coasting through calm waters, your life is in a good state. If you're sailing expertly through tricky

conditions, or in charge of a lot of people onboard, rest assured that all is well. If your boat is capsizing, then you need to take this lesson into your waking life; learn new skills before taking risks.

SAINT

Whether or not you are of a religious nature, if you see a saint in your dream, then it's likely that you are ready to receive a profoundly spiritual message. The "saint" is the part of your subconscious mind that is unified with everything. Listen and learn.

SALMON

To the Celts, the salmon is one of the most sacred animals, standing for wisdom and regeneration. Whatever your sensibilities, the salmon is a wonderful creature to encounter in your dream, especially if you find yourself in the shape of a salmon or swimming alongside one. To dream that you are a fish of any kind involves moving in a different dimension; effectively, it involves superhuman powers. Combine this with the symbolism of the salmon and be aware that you have access to just as much power in your waking life.

SALT

A highly valued substance in days gone by, we get a small idea of the importance of salt in that the word "salary" is derived from the same origins. Salt adds flavor to food, is used to cauterize wounds, and has a purifying effect. If you are eating salt in your dream, then there's something in your life that is good for you, but that you also find distasteful.

SAMURAI

If you dream you are a samurai, you could be feeling disempowered and frustrated in your waking life. Do as a samurai would—take control and do something about it!

SANDCASTLE

An archetypal image of a childhood summer, the sandcastle is washed away as soon as the ocean rushes over it. It might be that you are putting a lot of effort into something that doesn't really merit such attention. Enjoy what you're doing, but don't expect too much.

SANDWICH

Food generally represents spiritual nourishment, and if in your dream you're eating a sandwich, then it would imply that you're taking shortcuts in whatever spiritual practice you follow. Then again, maybe you're just hungry?

SANTA

There's a great deal of mystery surrounding the figure of Santa.

We warn children not to speak to strangers, but then encourage them to tell all their secrets to a fat man, dressed in red, and wearing a fake beard. Santa may speak to you of the innocence of childhood, or he may have a more sinister meaning in your dream. However, in general, the character represents surprises, magic, and generosity. This is all good, whether or not you believe in him.

SAUNA

If you feel comfortable in your dream sauna, naked or at least semiclad in the company of strangers, then this is a healthy sign that you're comfortable in your own skin, metaphorically speaking, in your waking life. If, on the other hand, you find yourself in a sauna fully dressed and uncomfortably hot, it could be that there are parallel aspects of your real life that are similarly uncomfortable. Ask yourself why this should be. Perhaps you should, figuratively speaking, take some clothes off and relax a little or alternatively change your environment.

SCAFFOLDING

Scaffolding provides stability for a fragile structure. Think about where you might need to apply such stability in your waking life.

SCARAB

Considered one of the most sacred creatures in Egyptian life, the scarab beetle represents the continuum of the sun and eternal life. This symbolism is so ancient as to be a part of our general consciousness. Are you having regular dreams of all things mysterious and Egyptian? Perhaps you're a reincarnated Pharaoh, in which case you might find that your waking life is rather uncomfortable and unfamiliar. Scarabs are also survivors, so it could indicate that your ability to weather distress and change.

SCHOOL

Ah, to dream that you're back at school (assuming that you have actually left). Some might say that their schooldays are the happiest of their lives, but for others this is certainly not the case, and such a dream might have a certain amount of anxiety attached that reflects a situation in your waking life: a dictatorial boss, a lack of responsibility, impending exams and tests? On the other hand, such a dream might imply a longing for a return to easier and more innocent times. You need to address whatever it is that's causing such sleep-time escapism.

SCISSORS

If you dream of giant scissors marching toward you, this has obvious, somewhat frightening, sexual connotations as the blades that open and close decisively represent legs. If you don't feel the dream was a sexual one in nature, then the scissors might be showing you that you need to cut out certain unhealthy aspects of your waking life.

SEAHORSE

The seahorse is an otherworldly, unusual creature that breaks all the rules of nature. Not only are they horses that live in the ocean, but it is the male that gives birth to offspring. If you are in the ocean among seahorses in your dream, or even dreaming that you

THE TEEN DREAMER WHO INVENTED FRANKENSTEIN

Frankenstein might seem to be the product of a nightmare, but in fact the character came to his creator via a dream. This dream would prove very lucrative to Mary Shelley, who was only 19 at the time she had the dream and wrote the story.

Mary Wollstonecraft Godwin, as she was then named, was visiting the poet, Lord Byron, with her lover, Percy Shelley. Byron's villa beside Lake Geneva was beset with bad weather, and the party were forced to spend time indoors, trying to find ways of entertaining themselves. Part of this entertainment included reading one another ghost stories, and Byron suggested that they should each try to write a new story. Mary describes very well the moment of her inspiration:

…When I placed my head upon my pillow, I did not sleep, nor could I be said to think… I saw—with shut eyes, but acute mental vision— I saw the pale student of unhallowed arts kneeling beside the thing he had put together. I saw the hideous phantasm of a man stretched out, and then, on the working of some powerful engine, show signs of life, and stir with an uneasy, half-vital motion. Frightful must it be; for supremely frightful would be the effect of any human endeavour to mock the stupendous Creator of the world.

…I opened mine in terror. The idea so possessed my mind, that a thrill of fear ran through me, and I wished to exchange the ghastly image of my fancy for the realities around. …I could not so easily get rid of my hideous phantom; still it haunted me. I must try to think of something else. I recurred to my ghost story—my tiresome, unlucky

ghost story! O! if I could only contrive one which would frighten my reader as I myself had been frightened that night!

Swift as light and as cheering was the idea that broke upon me. "I have found it! What terrified me will terrify others; and I need only describe the spectre which had haunted me my midnight pillow." On the morrow I announced that I had thought of a story. I began that day with the words, "It was on a dreary night of November," making only a transcript of the grim terrors of my waking dream...

The rest, as they say, is history. Even today the very word "Frankenstein" is synonymous with the idea of any horrible, uncontrollable, man-made monstrosity. And, by the way, Mary Wollestonecraft Godwin subsequently married Shelley.

actually are a seahorse, then you are being put in touch with your perceptive and psychic powers, learning to see the world from a totally different viewpoint. This is very good omen indeed, and you should relish such a dream.

SEASHELLS

Because seashells were once the "homes" of small creatures, and because you can hear the "sea" in them when you hold them to your ear, they're symbolic of hidden secrets. Is there something you're not telling someone, or something you feel they're not telling you?

SEEDS

A seed contains all it needs to transform into a plant. An tiny acorn is imbued with the power of the mighty oak tree that it will one day become. A seed of any description is full of potential, and to dream of a seed or seeds is to dream of new ideas and possibilities combined with all the adventure and excitement of a fresh start.

SEQUINS

To dream of sequins indicates that you are probably seeking more glamour in your waking life.

SEWER

A sewer transports waste material, so to dream of a sewer is to realize that you have waste material or '"baggage" that similarly needs to be removed from your life. This might include old ideas, bad habits, excess weight… You'll know what it is.

SEWING

The meaning depends on whether you're making something or repairing something. If it's the former, then your dream world is prompting you to express your creativity more in any context you care to mention. If the latter, then you are reaching a new kind of maturity and stability in your waking life.

SEX

This subject could of course merit an entire chapter all to itself, but let's keep it as simple as possible. Your sexy dream is making up for the lack of such shenanigans in your real life; your subconscious mind is telling you that you have natural urges and a thirst that has to be slaked; a hunger satisfied. Maybe you are having problems forming relationships, or perhaps you are repressed. Life is to be enjoyed. Seek therapy if necessary, but pay attention to your dream.

SHADOWS

First you need to establish what or who the shadows belong to. Then you need to know that the shadow symbolizes the "hidden" or alternative aspect of something. The shadow in your dream is yourself or a side of yourself that is about to come into the sunshine.

SHAMAN

The Shaman is a person who can act as a guide into the "world of spirit," and his or her intention is to help you gain a greater understanding of yourself, the world around you, and your own place in that world. Pay attention to the words and actions of the Shaman in your dream and view his or her appearance as a privilege.

SHEEP

Relating to compliance and conformity, your relationship to the sheep in the dream is important. If you are one of the flock, then it's likely you feel comfortable being part of a group. However, if you are you an outsider or the "black sheep," you might feel yourself to be at odds with the people you work with.

SHIP

If a house represents your state of mind and internal life, then a ship similarly represents the emotions, constantly shifting and journeying. The size of the ship and the waters it travels on should tell you the rest. It's self-evident that a shipshape ship sailing in calm waters means that all is well.

SHOES

An important symbol of your state of mind, if your dream shoes are comfortable and appropriate for your situation, you're on the right path. On the other hand, if the shoes are ill-fitting or inappropriate, then the opposite is true. Shoes are also a sexual symbol, a veiled allusion to the vagina.

SHOOTING STAR

To dream of a shooting star in your dream is to know that fabulous, exciting, and new opportunities are lining themselves up for you.

SHORELINE (See Beach)

SHOWER

If the shower in your dream consists of muddy or dirty water, then there are emotions and feelings that you need to offload, pronto. If the water is clean and clear, however, you're in a healthy state of mind. If you're sharing a shower with someone, then you have a confession to make.

SHRINKING

Sometimes items that appear in your dreams are much bigger or smaller in size than you expect them to be in everyday life. Lewis Carroll used this idea of shrinking down objects to great effect in his infamous book, *Alice's Adventures in Wonderland*. If you dream that you yourself are much too small, then you could be feeling overlooked and ignored in some waking matter. If certain objects are too small, pay attention to what these items are; they are no longer as relevant in your life as they once were.

SIGN LANGUAGE

Sign language is an effective form of communication that is used primarily

FAMOUS FREAKY DREAMERS
THE DREAM MACHINE

Guess how the sewing machine was invented? Yes, that's right; the key component of the machine came to its inventor, Elias Howe, in a dream. Howe had an idea for a machine that would make stitching cloth faster and more efficient than sewing by hand, but finding a way to make the needle work in the machine was proving to be a real dilemma. He'd tried a needle that was pointed at both ends with the eye in the middle, but it was a disaster. Subsequent ideas were going nowhere, and Howe was about to ditch the whole concept when he had a dream that solved the problem. In the dream, angry natives had taken him prisoner (presumably in a jungle) and were shaking their pointy spears at him. Eureka! Even in the midst of his fear, Howe noticed that the spears had holes near their sharp tips. This was exactly the inspiration he needed to make his sewing machine viable. Genius!

by deaf people. Since it is not a language known by all, to dream of sign language is an indication that not everyone will "get the message." It could mean that in your waking life there may be crossed lines of communication or misunderstandings that need to be corrected.

SKATING

If you are learning to skate (either roller or ice) in your dream, then you are learning new skills in a relatively alien environment. Are you skating beautifully? In this case, given that many dreams show us an ideal situation that is the opposite of our waking experience, it's possible that you are struggling with some feature of your waking life. Nevertheless, the dream indicates that you know what you need to do to fix things, so get going.

SKIPPING

Skipping indicates a lighthearted attitude, an activity primarily of children. Dreams can sometimes throw curveballs of meaning at us, so you're not feeling particularly lighthearted, then your dream could be telling you

that you've "skipped" out on something that's either essential or obvious.

SLEEPING

To dream that you're sleeping seems like the ultimate waste of time, but it does happen occasionally. Generally speaking, this means that you're in calm control of your life, although things might be becoming a little tedious. If you see someone else sleeping, you might be worried about health matters or even death, either specifically about that person or generally. To dream that you're dreaming is a different matter altogether (*See* page 156 for further information on **Lucid Dreaming**).

SLIPPING

To dream that you're slipping and sliding suggests that there's cause to be concerned with your waking stability, though not necessarily physical stability. It could also be an indication of your emotional and mental states.

SLOW MOTION

A slow-motion dream, where it feels as though you're wading through molasses, means that your mind is working much faster than those around you. Ask yourself whether it's because you're feeling held back or somehow frustrated by those around you in your waking life.

SMILING

If people are smiling at you and looking pleased in your dream, it's likely that you might be missing this kind of interaction in your waking life. If you feel yourself to be smiling, however, then it's likely you're just having a rather lovely dream.

SMOKE

Ancient humans believed that smoke of any kind carried messages and prayers to their gods as it spiraled upward toward them. That's why Native Americans smoked the pipe of peace, and why incense is still used in rituals across all religions, from Catholicism to Wicca. Maybe you are communicating with your own gods? Smoke is also an indicator that there's a fire smoldering somewhere; this could be the fire of a new idea that has yet to gain momentum. Or perhaps the house is on fire.

SNAKE

The snake or serpent has obvious sexual connotations, and is also unfortunate enough to be associated with treachery after its tussle with Adam and Eve. Connected to all things earthly because of its proximity to the ground, if you see a snake in your dream, it's likely that you too need to be "earthed". This can include looking at your health and diet, as well as your sexual life. The snake could also represent someone who is up to no good, depending on its behavior in the dream.

SNOW

The whiteness, texture, and drifting patterns of snow suggest purity, beauty, and a fresh start. If the snow is dirty, there's some aspect of your waking life that you're very unhappy with, that you feel is holding you back. If you are caught in a snow drift, it could be that matters are getting on top of you or you could be feeling swamped by others' good intentions.

SPACESHIP

A spaceship in your dream implies that anything is possible, the sky's the limit, and that new, unexplored horizons await you. If the spaceship is full of aliens and everything seems a little too real for comfort, however, then it's possible that you're being abducted in real life. Try to bring something back with you that will bear forensic examination.

SPHINX

The stony face of the Sphinx suggests the mystery of the unknown and an element of danger. If you dream of the Sphinx, then there's a possibility that in your waking life you have some kind of a connection to the past, and a chance to right some wrongs, or throw new light and understanding on certain matters.

SPIDER

Most people are afraid of spiders and when they appear in a dream, they encourage us to face any irrational fears. The bigger the spiders are in size, the more illogical these fears are. (*See* **Web**.)

SPIRAL

The seemingly never-ending spiral shape represents infinite possibilities and your own burgeoning creative energies, reminding you that you are capable of anything. Enjoy!

SQUIRREL

Squirrels are often symbolic of hard work, as they harvest their food stores in the fall. A dream about squirrels might mean that you are working hard to no avail. It's possible that you're wondering about the meaning of life or that the squirrel in your dream is showing you that there's another way, and that all is not lost.

STAGE

If you are acting on a stage in your dream, consider what it feels like. Are you happy to be the star of the show, or do you wish the ground would swallow you up? The stage represents your life as it is right now, so the rest should be self-evident. If you dream that you're watching others on a stage, it's possible that you are feeling slightly detached from your own life.

STARS

Are you seeing stars? This is a good sign, as stars represent the fulfillment of hopes, ideals, and aspirations. The more stars you see in your dream, the merrier.

STORK

Traditionally, the stork brings babies. It may be that you're pregnant, or thinking of starting a family, or alternatively, these "babies" can represent ideas or new beginnings.

STRANGER

Observe the stranger in your dream very closely. He or she represents an aspect of yourself that you have hitherto not been aware of, and this could be quite an exciting prospect. Perhaps this stranger has a talent for something that you'd never dreamed of, and your dream could be telling you that you are more versatile than you think.

SUGAR

If you are eating sugar in your dream, then you need to experience more "sweetness" in your waking life.

SWAN

The pure white beauty and calm demeanor of the swan as she glides across the water belies an awful lot of paddling commotion underneath the water. Perhaps this is how you're feeling at the moment. It's OK to ask for help should you need it!

TABLE

A table is essentially a piece of furniture with four legs, but it's also a focal point for people. The Round Table of King Arthur was the symbol of the fellowship that met around it. Whether the emphasis is on business meetings, meals, or a simple cup of coffee, the table is a central point for gatherings and is therefore a symbol of unity. If the table in your dream is wobbly or off-center, then there might similarly be issues with the relationships between the people that use that table.

TACK *(See* **Nails***)*

TAIL

Have you suddenly grown a tail in your dream? This would suggest that your animal nature is keen to reveal itself to you. If you can go as far as identifying the type of tail, then you'll know which animal this is (hopefully not a mouse).

TALENT CONTEST

If you're starring in a talent contest in your dream, then you know that it's also time to show off your talents in real life. These might not be of the singing/dancing variety; nevertheless, whatever you've got, it's time to flaunt it.

TAMING

If you're taming a wild animal, take note of what type of animal it is. It might be time to embrace the animal part of yourself or the character traits of that particular creature. However, if, for example, you're a wild dog inside, it's probably best not to urinate against trees in public.

TANDEM BICYCLE

The symbolism of riding in tandem with someone is pretty self-explanatory, suggesting an equal partnership and teamwork. You may find, though, that one of you is freewheeling, meaning that the person isn't pulling their weight in real life.

TANGLES

Any kinds of tangling—hair, rope, wires—indicate confusion and obstacles in your waking life. The nature of what is tangled should tell you where those hindrances lie. Tangled hair, for examples, relates to confused ideas due to a lack of clear thinking.

TAPESTRY

A dream tapestry is made up of little stitches that, when combined, all contribute to the bigger picture. So whether you're dreaming of an actual sewn tapestry, or a metaphorical "tapestry," the state will tell you much about your own attitude to life.

TAROT CARDS

If tarot cards mean anything to you at all and you read them or have had readings done for you in the past, then it's likely that you will have some idea of what the dream is telling you. However, the images and symbols of the tarot are so archetypal that just about anyone will be able to deduce the meanings of the cards. If you dream that you are reading the cards for someone else, it's likely that you have wisdom or advice to offer them.

TATTOO

First determine if the tattoo is on you or somebody else in the dream. Tattoos suggest permanence and

individuality. If the tattoo is of a bird or animal, you should think about the qualities or symbolism implied in that animal and embrace those same qualities in yourself. If in real life you find the idea of tattoos to be repugnant, then the dream could be suggesting that you start looking at things in a different way. Tattoo dreams could also be showing you a message, and it is dependent on the nature of the tattoo is understand that message.

TEA

Drinking tea signifies harmony and unity, since many people share tea from one pot. If you are taking part in an ancient tea ceremony, then you may be thinking about a return to rituals and traditions in your waking life. These may belong to the trappings of conventional religion or to a spiritual tradition that's perhaps less orthodox.

TEACHER (TEACHING)

A teacher is a figure of authority and may relate to how you feel about a particular person in your waking life. Are you involved with teachers from day to day? If in your dream you are teaching, but you're not actually a member of this profession, you might feel that you have a lot of information to offer but that no one is listening. Why not try and change your approach to get others to pay attention? If you dream that you are being taught something, then think about what lessons you might actually still have to learn and who is teaching you.

TEDDY BEAR

A symbol of childhood and comfort, a teddy bear means that a part of you wants to go back to those innocent days of no responsibilities. Keep the happy memories, but get real—it's impossible to go back. (*See* **Bear**.)

TEETH

(*See* **Popular Dreams** on page 80).

TELEKINESIS

In your dream, are you able to make objects move using only the power of your mind? It's a thrilling feeling and it could be that you're on the edge of lucid dreaming (*See* page 156). Or it could

indicate that you have huge reserves of untapped potential that you need to start to use.

TELEPATHY

In your dream you might be telepathic, but you don't need to be telepathic in real life to get a handle on what people are thinking. The dream is telling you to try listening more in your waking life.

TELEPHONE

Sometimes our subconscious mind, bored of trying all sorts of tricks to try to get through to us, resorts to something very, very obvious in our dreams—the telephone. If you find yourself on the phone in your dream, pay close attention to what's being said and to what you, yourself, are saying.

TENT

If you find yourself in a tent in your dream, it could be that you're feeling a bit insecure about your real-life home environment—tents are impermanent, flimsy structures, after all. Then again, it might just be time for a vacation...

TERMITE

Destructive little varmints, those termites. They might be small, but they sure can take apart a building fast. To dream of a termite or a termite colony means that you're being made aware of the power of the old adage "a little at a time." Bear this in mind in your own life—but be aware that the results can be constructive as well as destructive.

TEST

(See Examination on page 83 and Popular Dreams on page 80)

TESTICLES

Did you know that the word "testament" derives from the same root as the word "testicles," and it used to be common practice among the ancient Romans to grab their balls when making a promise? That's because the testicles are such a vitally important part of the body. To dream of testicles is to be put in touch with masculine sexuality, no matter what your gender.

TEXTING

There's no way a few years ago that "texting" would have merited an entry in a book of dream symbols, but it's astounding how swiftly our minds become accustomed to new technology. It's particularly appropriate, really, since texts, like dreams, are about messages and information, so try to remember the specific words that feature in your dreams. The abbreviated language of texts is also well suited to dream language.

THANKSGIVING

A dream of Thanksgiving will usually involve family and friends gathered together at home to share food, conversation, laughter, and happiness. To dream about this holiday could indicate that you're missing this sort of interaction in your waking life. Perhaps it's time to get in touch with your loved ones and relatives; there's no need to wait until a holiday.

THIRST

Thirst in a dream might mean that you're craving a glass of water in your sleep, but metaphorically speaking it means that you're thirsting for something else—usually a spiritual slaking. Examine this spiritual part of your life and get to it!

THORNS

A thorny problem is a difficult one and this could be what you're facing in your dream. Thorns also afford a form of protection and you may be feeling like you need to protect yourself from something in your waking life.

THRESHOLD

A threshold isn't just the bit between the outside and the inside; it's any transitional place. A beach is a threshold and so is a rail station—in a dream, a threshold implies a similar "holding" area, a transition between two states of mind, two places, even two relationships.

THRONE

If you are sitting on the throne in your dream, you're afraid to embrace new responsibilities and ready to assume new powers. If, however, you're looking at an empty throne, then you know that you're not ready for it yet.

TIGER

Any animal that appears in a dream is usually an aspect of you, revealing its presence in a symbol. A tiger is a particularly powerful beast, and this kind of dream is likely telling you that you have access to that tiger-power.

TOAST

We sometimes say that something is "toast" if it's finished or done with, therefore, it could mean that there is something in your life that's "toast." Otherwise, this humble grilled bread speaks of simple pleasures.

TOBACCO

To the Native Americans, tobacco was a sacred herb, intended for communication with the Spirit World. Sadly, tobacco these days has assumed a much more mundane—not to mention, dangerous—reputation. Your own attitude toward smoking will inform what you make of your tobacco-laden dream.

TOES

What do the toes in your dream look like, and are they yours or someone else's? Our toes help us move through life; when we say that someone "keeps on their toes" we mean that they are awake and alert to any opportunity. Are you switched on to any opportunity? The state of your dream toes will lead you to the truth.

TOMATOES

The red color of the tomatoes tells you that you're in fine fettle. If, however, you're being pelted with rotten tomatoes in your dream, question what you might have done in your waking life to merit this?

TOMBS AND TOMBSTONES

It can be creepy to come across a tombstone in your dream—and even more horrifying to find that it has your name on it. When you wake, you may be filled with dread at the thought of the time that you have wasted and the opportunities that you have missed. In this case, such a dream is doing you a favor since you're still alive and have the opportunity to change things. And the actual tomb symbolizes parts of yourself that you have locked away. Is it time to dig those parts out?

TONGUE

How does the tongue appear in your dream? Meaning is all down to the context. Practitioners of Chinese medicine gauge the state of someone's health by examining their tongue. It's also considered extremely impolite in some parts of the world to stick your tongue out at someone. The tongue contains receptors that can distinguish between different tastes. The tongue is also an important instrument of sexual arousal, and a crucial part of the talking process. Has the cat got your tongue? Time to speak out!

TOPLESS

(*See* Popular Dreams on page 80)

TORPEDO

A blunt instrument related to masculine energy and power, the torpedo is an extremely powerful and destructive piece of equipment. Perhaps you're riding astride a torpedo—in which case, you are in control of that power.

TORTOISE

The fable of the tortoise and the hare is all about how the diligent plodder wins the race against the impulsive, reckless, and arrogant hare. This can be a good lesson to apply to your own life. However, occasionally we need a little reckless arrogance to spice things up.

TORTURE

Are you being physically tortured in a dream? Maybe you're in a medieval dungeon, chained down as you're lashed by a cat o'nine tails. Or perhaps the torture is something less painful, such as having your feet tickled with a feather. Sometimes these are the sorts of dreams that are so difficult to endure that our mind forces us awake. It could be that you're feeling powerless in your waking life; that you're being punished for some action. If you dream that you're inflicting torture on others, however, you need to be aware of the effect that your own actions can have on those around you. You may not see what you're doing in your waking life as being torture; others might.

TOURIST

Are you a stranger in an unfamiliar place, but feeling ready for adventure and exploration? An exciting position to be in. Perhaps your waking life is in need of such excitement, a change of scene, or a step into the unknown.

TOWER

A symbol of power, the state of the tower will reveal the condition of your own strength. The tower can also be a phallic symbol and could be a sign of sexual longing.

TOYS

Toys are the province of the pure, unadulterated, fertile, and wholly imaginative mind—i.e., that of a child. To play with toys in a dream marks a return to such a fresh and unadulterated way of thinking. Try and carry this attitude through to your waking life. Broken toys, on the other hand, can mean shattered dreams or disappointments.

TRAFFIC

The flow of the traffic reflects the "flow" of your normal, waking life. If the dream is full of massive trucks and other vehicles blocking your route on the freeway, then your life is similarly frustrated.

TRAFFIC LIGHTS

Whatever the color shown on the traffic light, the traffic light itself represents a greater authority that's in charge. Does this signify another person in your own life?

"There's a flock of bats coming toward me with human skull faces. They pick me up and take me flying with them, and I realize I'm one of them, come to scoop up the souls of the dying and take them to a kind of bat-hell that looks just like a bus station."

TRAIN

A form of transportation, but one that affords you little choice other than to finish the journey at the same destination as everyone else. Perhaps you feel trammeled in your waking life by a similar situation? A train going through a tunnel is also a commonly accepted sexual symbol—perhaps there's something missing in your life?

TRANSVESTISM

Whatever your sexual orientation, sometimes it's interesting to experience a different point of view. Since women can quite easily wear mens' clothes without anyone batting an eyelid, transvestism generally applies to men wearing ladies' clothes. Maybe you need to gain a different perspective in your everyday waking life.

TREES

Trees are symbols of longevity, the natural world, and wisdom. What sort of a tree do you see in your dream? It could represent an aspect of yourself (see Oak, Yew). If you're climbing a tree or at the top of a tree, then your life is going well and you're succeeding in your ambitions. If the tree is huge and rambling with many branches and places to hide, you're full of ideas and many talents. If you're in a tree house, then you're fully integrated into the natural world and the man-made one.

TUNNEL

The most obvious symbolism for the tunnel, seen in a dream, is of the vagina. You could be longing for sexual contact the desire revealing itself in the imagery in your dream. It can also speak of the birth process.

TWINS

The appearance of twins, in a dream, can represent an aspect of yourself. This aspect may be harmonious, or the twins might be at odds with one another. This might mean that you have conflicting opinions about something in your life or you may be in two minds about which course to take.

UFO

An Unidentified Flying Object (UFO) is not always a spaceship; however, this tends to be the most likely connection. To dream of a UFO reflects a desire for the unknown and a longing to escape from everyday cares and concerns. Sigh.

UGLINESS

To dream of unacceptable ugliness in yourself or in others means that there are aspects of your waking life—not necessarily to do with physical appearance—that need to be closely examined and, if necessary, removed.

UMBILICAL CORD

This is the cord that attaches us to things; initially to the mother figure during pregnancy, but it can also symbolize anything else that we are closely connected to. The umbilical cord also gives us a spiritual connection to the universe. It is also true to say that the umbilical cord has a short shelf life and it could be that you need to sever a stultifying attachment. (*See Navel*).

UMBRELLA

An umbrella provides shelter against adverse weather—what troubles are you experiencing in your waking life that you need shielding from? The word also implies a group of similar organizations, come together because of strength in numbers. Would such a sheltering organization be useful in your waking life?

UNDERGROUND

If you are traveling by the subway, i.e., underground, then you might be having one of those boring dreams that simply reflect your everyday life, or, then again you could be making surreptitious moves to change your life. Anything in a dream that is "under" or "below" speaks of the subconscious mind, and so the symbols and signs that you see in such a dream will be particularly meaningful. If you are working underground in some capacity, this means that your subconscious mind is happily integrated with your fully conscious thought processes.

UNDERTAKER

A death or an ending is occasionally signified by this gloomy character, but far from indicating real-life death, this type of figure in your dream can be viewed as heralding a new beginning. Not so gloomy after all?

UNDERWATER

Are you operating in an underwater environment? Water represents the emotions, so it's possible that you are feeling overwhelmed with your own feelings. You need to examine why this should be and do everything you can to get your life back on an even keel.

UNDERWEAR

Oops! Are you dreaming that you are only wearing your underwear in public? Then you probably feel embarrassed and ashamed, but in fact all that's happening is that a part of you that is normally hidden is being shown. Perhaps in your waking life you're being asked to show a part of yourself that you normally shy away from revealing. We're all the same under those clothes—go for it!

UNICORN

This mythical animal represents purity and high ideals. Traditionally, the unicorn could only be approached by a young virgin, so if you are able to approach the animal, then you're longing for a return to simplified, unsullied values and ideals. To dream that the unicorn is slaughtered means that you have to wave goodbye to something in the past that has been haunting you.

UNICYCLE

Are you spinning along with ease on a unicycle? If so, this indicates ultimate confidence and ability. However, if you're wobbling along, this means that you need to do a little groundwork before tackling a new project. Then again, you might be considering joining the circus!

UNIFORM

Do you need to wear a uniform in your working life? If so, to dream of a restrictive uniform signifies that you're in need of a change. If you don't normally wear a uniform, perhaps you long for security and conformity in your work. To wear a uniform is to sublimate your own personality to an extent, so you might want to think about whether there is something you want to hide.

UPSIDE DOWN

Things are often upside down, topsy-turvy, or otherwise reversed in dreams. This type of dream is reminding you to look at things in a different way, from a different point of view, and this new outlook may reveal new truths.

URINATING

Do you dream that you're urinating in the wrong place—in public, perhaps? Considered an embarrassing taboo, try to remember that this is only a dream. Are there other things that you might be feeling ashamed of in real life?

VACATION

Do your close friends and associates call you a workaholic? To dream that you're on vacation is a rather extreme form of wishful thinking. Your subconscious mind is telling you that you need to take a break. If you dream that you're having a horrendous vacation, this could be due to your anxiety about taking a break at all; you're trying to convince yourself the whole thing is a bad idea.

VALENTINE'S DAY

Are you dreaming that it's Valentine's Day and you haven't received any cards? You're feeling unloved and anxious, and this is reflected in your dream. The odd thing is that if you dream that you're receiving lots of cards, then you're in need of more love and affection in your waking life. If you dream that you are sending Valentine's cards, on the other hand, then you need to acknowledge the object of your desire more openly—this may be a person, an object, or a position that you covet. Be more upfront about what you want from your life.

VAMPIRE

If death and sex are closely related, then the vampire is the epitome of such a connection. The vampire seduces its victim and makes him (or her) a member of its own unholy club by piercing the skin of the neck and slurping up the blood. The term "vampire" has come to mean any person who saps the energy or will of another. Vampires have a legendary fear of garlic and crucifixes and can only be destroyed by a silver bullet or a stake through the heart. If you dream that you are a member of this exotic tribe, it's possible that you are feeling impotent and maybe a little boring in your everyday life. If you dream that you are being pursued by a vampire, you need to face up to your sensual and erotic side. Or it could also indicate that there is someone in your life who is wasting all your time and energy.

THE VAMPIRE THRILLER

It wasn't just Mary Wollstonecraft that took inspiration from a dream for her famous literary monster, Frankenstein. Anne Rice—well-known for her hair-raising vampire tales—regularly uses her shut-eye time to dream up plots and characters. Anne's day dreams are particularly inspiring.

Here's an extract from Naomi Epel's *Writers Dreaming*. Here, Anne Rice describes how she became one of her most famous dream creations, the vampire, Lestat:

In a recent dream...I was one of my characters. I was the vampire Lestat, my hero. I was trying to go up the side of a castle. I threw a star-shaped thing, way up in the air so that it held fast to the side of the battlements. Then I climbed the rope that was attached to it. This was a very very vividly shocking dream.

About six months later, at the Frankfurt Book Fair, my German publishers took me to Heidelberg and there I saw this castle. It was really a shock, because the castle appeared to have exactly the same type of facade as the one that Lestat had climbed in the dream...

That Anne Rice's dream was shortly corroborated by reality makes the Freaky Dreams Freakometer shoot right up to number 11.

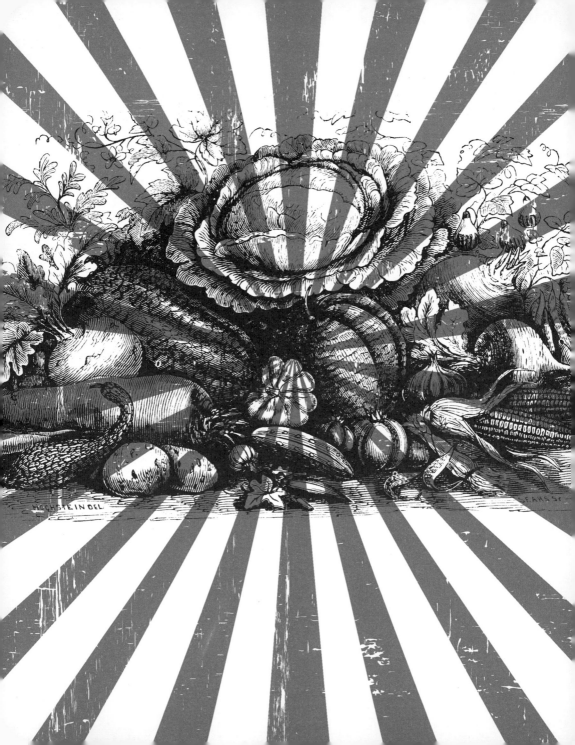

VASE

A container that holds any kind of liquid is usually related to the feminine element—and a vase that holds flowers amplifies this connection with femininity. If the vase is empty, then your dream is telling you that you need to connect with this female energy.

VEGETABLES

Any form of nourishment relates to your spiritual life and any type of plant often relates to the same concept. So vegetables represent a virtual double whammy of spirituality. Then again, some vegetables have phallic connotations and are more connected to sexuality than spirituality. The condition of the vegetables will tell you all you need to know. If these dream vegetables are being presented as a harvest, then you are reaping the rewards of meaningful endeavors.

VEHICLE

The Hindu gods are often associated with animals that are said to be their "vehicles." In the same way, you are closely identified with whichever vehicle you are riding in your dream. If it's a tatty old car, for example, you're not at all bothered by material objects or status symbols. If it's a huge pantechnicon, you need to feel powerful. If it's a motorcycle, you relish your freedom and singular nature.

VEIL

A veil is used to hide or conceal something. The veil of a bride, lifted at the point of marriage, refers to the breaking of the hymen—so, you see, this simple filmy piece of cloth has a much richer meaning. If you are veiled in your dream, then you are hiding some aspect of yourself. If you are approached by a person wearing a veil, then something is being concealed from you. If a veil is lifted, then you gain access to great secrets—whether or not you can remember what these secrets are on waking, however, is another matter entirely.

VENTRILOQUIST

The ventriloquist and his doll might signify that your subconscious mind is trying to give you a message. Pay close attention to what the ventriloquist is saying and to the nature of the doll. Sometimes these little characters can be quite sinister as a message-giving middleman.

VENUS FLYTRAP

These sinister, meat-eating plants denote voracious female energies. It could relate to a female in your life who is best avoided. Or it could relate to an aspect of your own personality that needs to be kept under control.

VINES

Are the vines in good condition, dripping with ripe grapes? If so, this is a wonderful dream symbol. Abundance, joy, freedom, fun, fertility—all are yours for the picking. If, however, the grapes are withered or the vines tattered and leafless, then you have regrets about wasting your time and talents. This dream, though, is telling you that it's never too late to turn over a new leaf and make a fresh start.

VIOLETS

The shrinking violet is a sign of shyness or a retiring nature. Violets are also dainty and fragrant little flowers. Perhaps these traits are similar to your own, or are you feeling fragile, easily crushed, with your beauty overlooked?

VIRGIN MARY

Or the BVM (Blessed Virgin Mary), as she is commonly called. It might be quite a thing to encounter her in a dream, particularly if you're a Catholic. She is the Great Mother, the feminine element of selflessness and purity. Maybe these are all qualities that you feel may be lacking in your life? Perhaps the BVM has a message for you. Listen carefully and consider the context in which she presents herself.

"I had a dream that my old grandma—who isn't actually dead—gave me the winning lottery numbers, all except for the final one. I wrote down the numbers on waking and bought ten tickets, all with a different number on the end. I didn't win, but what's odd is that Grandma actually did, and she'd only bought a ticket (using completely random numbers) because I told her about the dream!"

VISITOR

If you're receiving a visitor in your dream, this implies there is some important news coming to you in real life. Is the visitor male or female? Keep a note of this dream to see if the prophetic nature of it is indeed accurate.

VOLCANO

Carries much of the same meaning as an avalanche or a dam—there's a build-up of emotion that has no choice but to explode in a welter of molten debris.

VOMITING

Are you vomiting in your dream? There is some aspect of your waking life that needs to be purged from your system. Vomit in dreams is often not the same sort of substance as it is in real life, and its nature might give you a clue as to what needs to be done to make your existence a whole lot happier. It could even be in reference to a habit, such as smoking.

VOODOO DOLL

Someone is wishing you ill—or alternatively, you yourself might be the ill-wisher.

VULTURE

The circling vulture is a symbol of death, but also of recycling and renewal. There could be something in your life which is well past its sell-by date—perhaps a relationship. Throw it to the vultures and replace it with something way more interesting and useful.

WAITING ROOM

A luminal, threshold place, the waiting room is a neutral space between two other places. The waiting room in your dream can symbolize a transitional state between relationships, jobs, etc. as well as between physical places.

WALKIE-TALKIE

Dreams are the way that your subconscious mind processes experiences and information and gives messages and information. Sometimes the method of communication is obtuse; sometimes it's very straightforward. The interesting aspect of a walkie-talkie dream is that there's a possibility for two-way communication.

WAITER/WAITRESS

Are you waiting tables in your dream? It's likely, then, that in real life you are giving too much attention to the demands of others rather than taking care of your own needs. Whether those needs are for material goods, more time to pursue hobbies, or simply making your own choices about how you spend your time, get things into perspective.

WALKING

Are you on a long walk in your dream? Is it arduous? Do you wish it was over? Or are you enjoying it immensely, perhaps in good company? The walk here indicates your journey through life and your attitude to it, possibly more profoundly than "journey" dreams that involve a vehicle of some kind.

WALKING STICK

If you're using a walking stick in your dream when you don't need to use one in your everyday life, then perhaps you need to ask for assistance in some matter. Don't be afraid to ask for this help.

WALLS

Walls are generally barriers between two places; inside and outside, between two different rooms, a protective surrounding for a prison, castle, or fortress. Walls can keep you out or hold you in. If the walls in your dream are oppressive—which is usually the case—then circumstances in your own life might echo this sentiment. It might even be that the walls appear to be closing in on you, or that they are keeping you from an object of desire. Consider whether or not this feeling might be a reflection of your own thoughts and attitudes to certain aspects of your life.

WAND

Wouldn't it be great if, in real life, magic wands really worked? If you're wielding such an implement in your dream, with fantastic results, then, unfortunately, it's likely that in real life you seek to gain power of some kind in order to achieve what you need or to get what you want. Don't wait for a magic wand to arrive, because it's not going to happen.

WAR

A frightening dream, to find yourself mixed up in a war of some kind. Does the chaos, violence, and confusion reflect a situation in your waking life? If so, you need to take a step back and remove yourself, metaphorically speaking, from the battlefield.

WARDROBE

To dream that you're hiding in a wardrobe shows a desire to return to a safe, secure, innocent childhood environment. If the wardrobe is full of exotic and luxurious clothes, there are obvious sexual connotations. You may be feeling a lack of sensual comfort in your waking life.

WAREHOUSE

To dream that you're in a warehouse indicates that you're in a "holding pattern" in your waking life; perhaps you're between relationships, jobs, homes, or countries even. You might find that the contents of the lofty warehouse represent all the material detritus of life that you no longer have any use for. Perhaps it is time to offload some of it.

WARNING

If you receive a clear warning in a dream it would be unwise to ignore it. The warning may not appear to be related to anything in particular—it might seem indeterminate. Meditation can help clarify the issue. The dream will usually contain enough symbolic information to tell you all you need to know.

WARRIOR

Do you dream that you're a warrior? It could mean that you're feeling powerless and perhaps somewhat impotent in your waking life and that you want to face this head on. To dream that you're facing a mighty warrior is to come to terms with your own power.

WART

A wart represents something about yourself that's considered to be unacceptable, but that isn't really so bad. This could be something that you fear will be abhorrent to others; some sort of disability or character defect. Best to let it all hang out and be who, and what, you are.

WASHING

Washing is to do with cleansing, not physically, but spiritually. However, repeated obsessive washing of the hands is indicative of guilt. (*See* **Water, Waterfall,** and **Whirlpool.**)

WASP

Annoying, dangerous, and not a whole lot of use to mankind, the wasp is generally regarded as a pest. We use the term "waspish" to describe someone who tends to be sharply witty, irritating, but intelligent with a bit of a sting. Does this sound like someone you know?

WATCH

To see any kind of time-telling device in a dream indicates a preoccupation with the time. This is the sort of dream you might have if you know that you need to get up earlier than usual, and you might be anxious that your alarm clock might not go off. You might also be concerned about the passing of time in general and, inevitably, your own mortality.

WATER

In all its aspects, water represents the female element and the emotions. Knowing this simple fact takes a whole lot of guesswork out of watery dreams. It means that all you have to do is observe the type of water, its condition, and its "temper." (*See* **Whirlpool** and **Waterfall**.)

WATERFALL

Knowing what we already know about water dreams (*see Water*) the waterfall has another aspect—it's about cleansing—spiritual cleansing, the sweeping away of all extraneous habits, negative thoughts, and outmoded belief systems. To dream that you're under a waterfall means that this super-cleansing process is already taking place on a psychic level. Lucky you!

WAVES

A gauge for your emotions, if the waves are smooth and evenly rolling, then your state of mind is equally calm. If, on the other hand ,the waves are rough and choppy, you're experiencing rough emotional weather.

WEALTH

What does wealth mean to you? Is it a simple amassing of material gain? NO. Is it to do with a large bank balance and money stashed in jars or under the mattress? NO. Is it about personal happiness, warm friends, a functional family, and a lot of love in your life?

YES. To dream of wealth might suggest that you're looking at things in the wrong way and that you need to sort out your priorities.

WEAPONS

Are you wielding weapons in your dream? If so, you're feeling powerless and somewhat impotent—maybe even angry—in your waking life. If weapons are being pointed at you, or used against you, you feel that you are being unfairly treated by either a person or within the context of a situation.

WEASEL

Remember that animals in dreams tend to reflect characteristics of ourselves, so you have to ask yourself what the weasel really means to you. Generally speaking, we think of weasels as being sly, sneaky, and dishonest. Are you trying to extract information from someone, in a less than straightforward manner? Or is someone trying to do this to you? This could be the "weasel" that is appearing in your dream.

WEATHER

The type of weather in your dream reflects your own emotional and psychic state, so interpretation of your weather dream should be self-evident. A sunny day implies a bright phase of your life, whereas gloomy, dull, or cloudy weather in your dream implies that aspects of your life are equally as miserable.

WEB

A cleverly woven and beautiful tool of entrapment, the web is a very necessary piece of survival equipment for the spider. For all its beauty, however, a web tends to have negative connotations. (*See* **Spider**.)

WEEDS

Weeds are perceived as being unwanted plants by most gardeners—plants that appear in the wrong place at the wrong time. To dream of weeds might suggest that there are aspects of your own life that are similarly useless and getting in your way.

WEREWOLF

What are the key feature of a werewolf? With the arrival of a full moon, it's someone who appears to be a normal human being transforming into a ravenous, wolflike beast with crazed red eyes and hairy hands. Is there someone around you that you don't quite trust? To dream that you yourself shape-shift into a werewolf implies that you have hidden powers and talents that you're afraid of.

WHIRLPOOL

Water is all about feminine energies, qualities, and emotions (*see* **Water**). The whirlpool therefore represents a tumultuous mental state; all your thoughts are whirling around in chaos and you're getting nowhere. You need to step back from this mental whirlpool, if you can, to gain perspective on a certain situation or relationship.

WHISKEY

This might be an intoxicating spirit, but symbolically it speaks of the magical power of transformation. If you're drinking whiskey in your dream, perhaps you want to be someone else for a while or explore other aspects of your character.

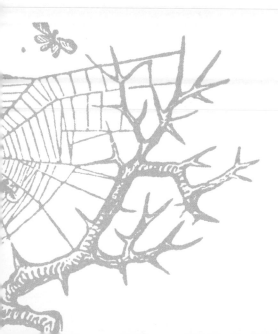

WIG

Wigs are symbolic of lies, deceit, and subterfuge. You may see someone that you know who is very obviously wearing a hairpiece. Are you absolutely sure that you trust this person in your waking life?

WIND

Wind might manifest itself in your dreams as a turning windmill, or wind chimes, or the trees bending toward the ground. Or you might be caught in a windstorm of some kind. Whatever form the wind takes, it symbolizes the conscious mind and the intellect. You might feel intuitively that something is not right, but your rational mind is overriding this intuition. The wind in your dream is a reminder that the intellect and the intuition can, in fact, work in tandem.

WINDOW

Are you outside, looking in at a window? Take notice of what you see, as this might represent something that you need in your life, whether you realize it or not. If you are inside, looking out of a window, you are longing for some kind of change in your circumstances.

WINGS

Do you have wings in your dream, but are unable to fly? This means that you have all the attributes you need, but that your own mental attitude is holding you back. Wings are symbolic of transcendence and divine communication, and the ability to "take flight" can refer to your spiritual and emotional life as well as your career. However, you don't need to have wings in order to fly in a dream. Flying is one of the most common dreams you can have. (*See* page 85 for more about **Flying** and other popular dreams.)

WITCH

Do you ever dream that you are a witch? If you do, then there's a side of yourself that you like to keep hidden—a side that you worry people will disapprove of. If you dream that a witch is talking to you or trying to interact with you, then the "magical" side of your personality—your instinctive and intuitive side—is trying to tell you something.

WOLF

Certain animals have such important meaning, and the wolf is one of these. A wolf stands for solitude, survival, ingenuity, resourcefulness, and intelligence; all qualities that you possess, but may need to unleash. Now you need to apply them in your waking life (without actually howling at the moon).

WOODS

Are you lost in a thickly wooded forest, unable to find the way out? The adage "can't see the wood for the trees" might be appropriate here if you feel beset by problems in life. However, try to see that irritations that might be forming a part of your life right now are essential to your growth as a material person and as a spiritual being. A dream about the woods could be indicating that you need to see opportunities, rather than problems.

WORM

Worms may be tiny, but they are an essential part of the infrastructure of Earth, and consequently of our planet. The worms in your dreams could be telling you to look after the little things and allow the big stuff to take care of itself.

WREATH

The circular shape of a wreath stands for unity and completion. The wreath itself symbolizes the material world, whereas the hole represents the Spirit World and that which is "unseen." If you dream that you're looking through the wreath, then you're interested in communication with that invisible world. We use wreaths as Christmas decorations and at funerals; if the wreath is made of flowers, then fresh blossoms signify a new start, whereas withered flowers are telling you that it's time to say goodbye to something or someone.

WRITING

Writing a letter is a sophisticated form of communication, and to dream that you are writing to someone might mean that in real life you're taking a roundabout way of telling that person something. Perhaps talking might be easier?

"I'm having a typical 'naked in public' anxiety dream, except the difference is that miniature sled dogs are eating away at my genitalia, and I can't show how nice it feels."

FAMOUS FREAKY DREAMERS
FROM NIGHTMARE TO BESTSELLER

When you think about it, sleep does sometimes seem to be a bit of a waste of time. Eight hours per night, 365 nights per year, for a life expectancy of 70 years—that's 204,400 hours of shut-eye, and approximately 23 years spent in the Land of Nod. Wouldn't it be great if all this sleep-time could yield some productivity for your waking life? Well, sometimes it happens.

Stephen King, renowned horror writer, talks about how his dreams often provide the inspiration for his stories. He has an interesting take on how he uses dreams, described in Naomi Epel's book *Writers Dreaming*:

I've always used dreams the way you'd use mirrors to look at something you couldn't see head-on, the way you use a mirror to look at your hair at the back. To me, that's what dreams are supposed to do. I think that dreams are a way that peoples' minds illustrate the nature of their problems. Or maybe even illustrate the answers to their problems in symbolic language.

Here he's talking about his book, *Misery*:
Like the ideas for some of my other novels, that came to me in a dream. In fact, it happened when I was on Concord. I fell asleep on the plane,

and dreamt about a woman who held a writer prisoner and killed
him, skinned him, fed the remains to her pig and bound his novel in
human skin. His skin, the writer's skin. I said to myself, "I have to
write this story." Of course, the plot changed quite a bit in the telling.
But I wrote the first forty or fifty pages right on the landing here,
between the ground floor and the first floor of the hotel.

King goes on;
Another time, when I got road-blocked in my novel It, I had a dream
about leeches inside discarded refrigerators. I immediately woke up
and thought, "That is where this is supposed to go." Dreams are just
another part of life. To me, it's like seeing something on the street
you can use in your fiction. You take it and plug it right in. Writers
are scavengers by nature.

XMAS

Is it Xmas in your dream? You are craving more fun and jollity in your life, and certainly a little more magic. Strive to create that Xmas feeling within no matter what the season and you'll find that things lighten up a little.

X-RAY

The thing about an x-ray is that it reveals the bare bones of a person or an animal. If you dream that you are undergoing such a treatment, how do you feel about it? Are you glad, or do you feel nervous about being exposed in this way? If you are administering the x-ray yourself, then it's likely that you need to analyze an area of your life quite closely. The dream might also be a warning of ill health.

XYLOPHONE

Think of the notes of the xylophone as having a similar symbolism to the rungs of a ladder; you can go up, or you can go down. Are you playing the xylophone? Can you remember what the tune is? These details may reveal a message.

YACHT

Are you sailing on a yacht in your dream? If so, the state of the yacht and the condition of the seas are key to its meaning. If it's a super-swanky luxury yacht zooming through calm seas, this is a great sign—indicating ease and fluidity. If the vessel is a bit tatty and struggling through choppy waters, it's not so good and you could be experiencing a struggle of some kind. Whatever the circumstances, this dream is telling you that you probably need to think about enjoying a little more leisure time.

YARN

There are two meanings to this word: yarn can be wool, or it can be a term used to describe a story or a tall tale. Perhaps you're knitting something. What is it that you're knitting— clothing? A scarf? This speaks of the need for you to express your creativity.

If you're spinning a yarn of a different sort, or listening to one, then you need to extend your imagination in this way in your day to day life—you need to look at things from a different perspective and take all circumstances into account.

YEAST

The effects of yeast can be quite magical. The natural yeasts in sugars are an important ingredient in turning grapes into wine and the yeast that's added to bread is what makes it rise. To dream of yeast is to dream of something that you take for granted that has a marked effect despite its seemingly humble status. This could be a person close to you or someone who has a "leavening" effect on your life.

YETI

Also known as the Abominable Snowman or Bigfoot, sightings of the yeti are rare and indeterminate. If you dream that you are tracking the yeti, then you could be following an almost impossible dream. If you dream that you are in close proximity to the yeti, then you are about to realize something very important.

YEW

Some trees are particularly symbolic, and the yew is one of these. The yew represents death as well as rebirth and resurrection. This is because of the great age that a yew tree can reach, as well as because of the way it grows. It breaks down and rots within the core of the trunk, from whose center the new shoots spring. Yew trees were considered to be so sacred that churches were often built where yew trees had grown. To dream of such a tree is to be connected with its ancient history and sacred status. It could also indicate that you too have undergone a great change in your life, but you are ready for a rebirth or resurrection of sorts.

YIN YANG

This is about the harmony and union of opposites, and if you dream of this sign, it's possible that you have been immersing yourself in Eastern philosophies. It may be that the balance indicated by the yin yang sign is something that you seek in your everyday waking life.

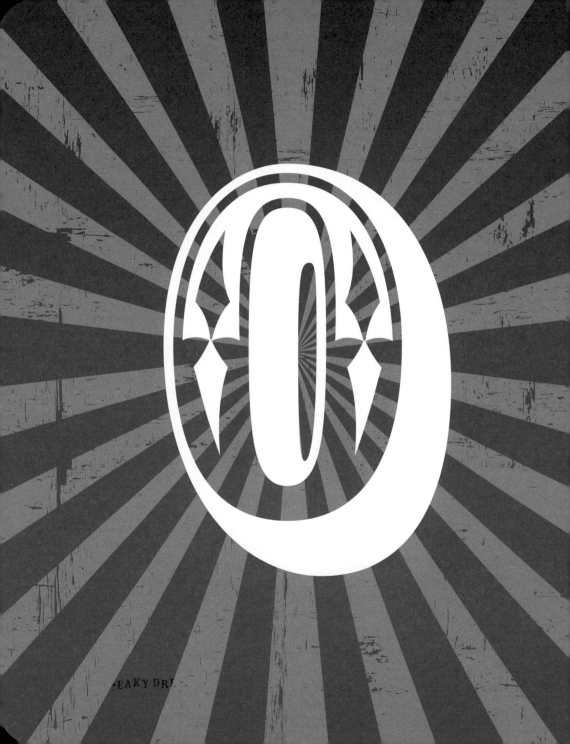

ZEBRA

They say that a zebra is just a horse in pajamas. But that's *so* wrong. They are very different animals, and the defining thing about the zebra is his black and white pop-art exterior. Graphically pleasing to the eye, the zebra symbolizes balance and harmony, as well as a little exotica.

ZERO

Is it a zero or is it a circle? Does a doughnut constitute a zero? Or a mouth shaping the letter "O"? If you're convinced that the big fat zero has appeared in your dream, then the shape stands for infinity and is, of course, much more than the sum of its parts—when added to the end of another number, the zero increases it tenfold. This dream could be telling you there's something in your life that's way more meaningful than you think.

ZIGZAG

The ups and downs of the zigzag symbol—often dramatic—are represented perfectly in the tracking on hospital monitor screens. Zigzag shapes in a dream reflect the fact that, in your waking life, you don't know whether you're coming or going... whether you're up or you're down.

ZODIAC

If you dream about the individual animals of the zodiac, you'll find their meanings under their respective entries. But to dream of the zodiac, that great wheel of stars personified as creatures and symbols, is to know that there is a world of mysteries out there for you to examine. This might seem daunting, but the effort will be worth it.

ZOO

If you're visiting a zoo in your dream, then the animals that you focus on most are those that bear a close relationship to your own character. To dream that you are an animal in captivity could mean that your full power has not yet been unleashed, or that part of you is effectively "caged"—perhaps that part of your personality has been held captive for a reason.

"I couldn't sleep, so I went downstairs and read for a bit, then went back to bed and fell into a state somewhere between sleeping and waking. Then, sort of floating in the air, I saw a man's face. He had a white mustache and hair, a beard, and a sailor's hat. I was transfixed with fear, and it felt as though I wasn't in charge of my body. I wanted to shout but I couldn't. I knew I wanted to fling myself out of bed to attract my sleeping girlfriend's attention, but I couldn't do that either. It was horrible."

NOTES

NOTES

NOTES

NOTES

NOTES

NOTES

NOTES

NOTES

NOTES

NOTES

NOTES

NOTES

NOTES

NOTES

NOTES